T0248266

From SCRAPPY to SELF-MADE

From
SCRAPPY
to
SELF-MADE

WHAT ENTREPRENEURS CAN LEARN
FROM AN ETHIOPIAN REFUGEE TO
TURN ROADBLOCKS INTO AN EMPIRE

YONAS HAGOS
with GARY M. STERN

NEW YORK   CHICAGO   SAN FRANCISCO   ATHENS   LONDON
MADRID   MEXICO CITY   MILAN   NEW DELHI
SINGAPORE   SYDNEY   TORONTO

1 2 3 4 5 6 7 8 9   LCR   28 27 26 25 24 23

ISBN   978-1-264-97021-6
MHID   1-264-97021-8

e-ISBN   978-1-264-96991-3
e-MHID   1-264-96991-0

Library of Congress Cataloging-in-Publication Data

Names: Hagos, Yonas, author.
Title: From scrappy to self-made : what entrepreneurs can learn from an
    Ethiopian refugee to turn roadblocks into an empire / Yonas Hagos with
    Gary Stern.
Description: New York : McGraw Hill Education, [2024] | Includes
    bibliographical references and index.
Identifiers: LCCN 2023016241 (print) | LCCN 2023016242 (ebook) |
    ISBN 9781264970216 (hardback) | ISBN 9781264969913 (ebook)
Subjects: LCSH: Hagos, Yonas. | Success in business—United States. |
    Entrepreneurship—United States. | Businesspeople—United States.
Classification: LCC HF5386 .H2146 2024 (print) | LCC HF5386 (ebook)
    | DDC 650.1—dc23/eng/20230608
LC record available at https://lccn.loc.gov/2023016241
LC ebook record available at https://lccn.loc.gov/2023016242

McGraw Hill books are available at special quantity discounts to use as premiums and sales promotions or for use in corporate training programs. To contact a representative, please visit the Contact Us pages at www.mhprofessional.com.

McGraw Hill is committed to making our products accessible to all learners. To learn more about the available support and accommodations we offer, please contact us at accessibility@mheducation.com. We also participate in the Access Text Network (www.accesstext.org), and ATN members may submit requests through ATN.

*I want to dedicate this book to
my wife, my kids, and my mom.
Thank you for all your support.*

CONTENTS

FOREWORD

When I was asked to share my experience working with Yonas, I was elated to reflect on who he is as a person, because Yonas is truly someone who displays the highest character and moral integrity through everything he does. Over the last four years, I have had the pleasure of getting to know him personally and professionally through his journey to becoming a multiunit operator with Smoothie King.

Yonas's personal story is one of perseverance and strength. He is an immigrant whose family made the incredibly difficult decision to flee war-torn Ethiopia to seek refuge in a camp in the Sudan and then came to the United States when he was nine years old. Then, following the events of September 11, 2001, he enlisted in the US Army, earning a Purple Heart fighting in Iraq.

After serving in the military, Yonas went on to begin what would ultimately become an incredibly successful career in restaurant franchising. I'll never forget my first meeting with Yonas. It was in Chicago, where I had traveled to see his new Smoothie King store.

What stood out then—and is still evident today—is how very involved Yonas is in every detail of his business. He knows the business inside and out, and as a bonus, he's also fun to be around. While I didn't know Yonas during his time in the military, I can tell he is still a soldier at heart: He understands the mission we're trying to achieve at Smoothie King, executes our brand standards flawlessly, and never breaks protocol. He is a servant leader. Yet he is also a visionary and someone I believe is the future of our brand.

As you'll soon see throughout this book, Yonas is inspirational. And he lights up a room (or, in this case, the pages) when he talks about his passions, whether it's his family, community, or business endeavors.

I think Yonas's secret is that he's a go-getter. He's not one to sit back and wait. If he finds something that works, he is going to replicate that proven process over and over again. He is the embodiment of everything we stand for at Smoothie King and works to inspire people to live a healthy and active lifestyle every day.

—Dan Harmon, President &
Chief Operating Officer,
Smoothie King

INTRODUCTION

What Entrepreneurs Can Learn from an Ethiopian Refugee to Turn Roadblocks into an Empire

Immigrants have a leg up on their competitors and most native-born people. Immigrants flock to America to work hard; that's why they come here. Not to take it easy. Not to rest. Not to have things handed to them. But to toil eight hours a day, and sometimes more, to get the job done, save some money, establish a roof over their head, become rooted in a community, and make their lives better, and most of all, improve the future of their children.

If you're willing to work tirelessly and play by the rules, the system works. And though capitalism has become a whipping boy for criticism because of certain built-in inequities, it operates like no other system. And for people who are enterprising, inventive, problem-solving, and ambitious, it continues to operate effectively, fairly, and equitably, in many cases.

When you are an entrepreneur, whether you were born in your country or emigrated from somewhere else, or work or live overseas, or are launching a business in any destination, roadblocks are inevitable. Putting yourself out there, many times on a creative or financial limb, means you are vulnerable to more failures than success, more challenges than smooth sailing, and many more questions than answers. As an immigrant, being an entrepreneur means taking the expected number of roadblocks and multiplying them tenfold. Language and culture barriers, lack of network or support, racial or cultural biases, lack of credit, and on and on, compound the already vulnerable place entrepreneurs put themselves in. I tell you this, not for pity or to whine in any way, but to explain why I think entrepreneurs can learn from immigrants who have also started and grown successful businesses. We found ways through the struggle, got inventive, had harder blows that we bounced back from, and can share that knowledge and journey to anyone with an entrepreneurial spirit.

And though my background and expertise are rooted in operating restaurant franchises and then independent eateries, this book is aimed beyond that narrow contingent. It's aimed at anyone who has an entrepreneurial spirit and wants to launch his or her own business. And it could be any kind of business, ranging from a cleaning-and-painting service (which as you'll see was my first venture out of the starting gate), a startup store, an app, a food truck, a dry-cleaning store, a bodega, a translation service, or just about anything else where one person (or perhaps more than one) is launching a shop, service, or business. It could even be a startup business ignited by an Instagram account, which is how one real estate agent introduced an online business for real estate brokers to generate leads.

This may sound like a platitude, but you need to find your passion. If golf is your passion, then consider opening a golf specialty store, or a golf-themed bar filled with golf memorabilia, or a golf training school. When I meet people who want to open a franchised restaurant because it will yield passive income, I know they're often doomed for failure. Making money isn't the same as being driven and energized by a love of something. It's just a capitalistic goal, and it will eventually, as I've seen ample times before, lead to failure and/or depression. Cliché or not, finding your passion is essential to launching your business dream—and sustaining it.

Once you've found your passion, educate yourself about the business to determine whether you're a good fit. That can entail working as a barista if the coffee business is your dream, or as a salesperson in a ski shop if opening a ski shop is your ultimate pursuit, or as a translator if you want to open such a business. Immerse yourself in the business, ask questions, find a mentor, and observe everything. It's what I did (which you'll see in future chapters) when I started as a teenager in entry-level roles at McDonald's and Burger King.

Become a sponge. Observe all you can see, and absorb everything. Focus on the specific details. How do orders come in? Whom are they ordered from? How are they priced?

A study titled "The National Study of Millionaires" by Ramsey Solutions published in April 2022 reported that only 21 percent of millionaires received any inheritance at all. That means four out of five millionaires earned their money on their own, likely emanating from modest means, and were self-made like myself. The notion that only the rich in the United States become millionaires is misguided and misinformed; most millionaires earn their money through hard work and determination.

Hence, you have to muster up and show true grit. Going beyond hard work, "grit" describes people who demonstrate perseverance toward a goal despite being confronted by various obstacles and distractions. Grit means overcoming hurdles, having the resolve to keep going, always believing in yourself, not giving up, not taking no for an answer, and showing the determination to keep going and never giving in.

Connected to that trait is showing "hustle." That means always finding ways to achieve your goals. Going beyond the call of duty. Stretching yourself to accomplish what you want to do.

Entrepreneurs come in all stripes and backgrounds and nationalities and ages. But in 2023, the landscape for starting a venture has been transformed. In the last few years, because the pandemic rattled and disrupted so many startup businesses, and money tightened up and interest rates rose, the marketplace has become more competitive and stratified. It's become harder to start a business and sustain it.

More and more, it takes a shark mentality to thrive as an entrepreneur. It's not that startup CEOs or founders need to attack anyone, but they need to attack problems, confront them, and devise solutions to them. When diners weren't permitted to eat inside a restaurant, we stepped up our drive-throughs, emphasized delivery, and engaged the services of third-party deliverers like DoorDash, Grubhub, and Uber Eats. And all restaurant operators had to enhance their websites, improve off-premises ordering, and increase social media marketing when their audience was staying home due to Covid restrictions.

In fact, startup entrepreneurs, whether restaurateurs, small-business owners, fitness instructors, or app developers, need to learn to attack problems before they even emerge. In 2023, before the year ended, I called all my district managers to ask them what they expected to be the major issue for the coming year, what was troubling them, what was leading to decreasing their revenue or disrupting their steady flow. For me, that's all part of the shark's entrepreneurial attitude: Attack the problem before it surfaces and grows.

When I think about my life and what it took to achieve my goals, I think about my 24-hour day. We all have the same hours in a day, whether born rich or dirt poor or somewhere in between.

How we choose what we do with that 24-hour period is what separates the winners and the entrepreneurial success stories from the others who fall by the wayside. I've also been able to make each 24-hour period pay off, never giving up, devoting my entire energy to meeting every challenge placed in front of me.

The 10 minutes you wasted staring into space, which can easily turn into an hour, you can never get back. Ultimately all we have in life is time. And I'm dedicated to making every minute count, with as few vacant moments as can be. Since time is our most valuable asset, I'm going to make the best of every minute, every hour, and every accomplish as much as I can. And that can entail owning 47 restaurant franchises, 2 independent eateries, a butcher shop, and a vodka company, all while nurturing a family—and who exactly knows what's next!

And that's a message I find that many people, including many 20-year-olds that I observe, don't seem to understand. What they do at that point in their emerging lives will determine the direction of their lives. Every minute counts, and their mindset can lead to creating the framework of their success. "Time cannot be wasted" is my motto, but must be taken advantage of, used, and contribute to one's impending success. Every lesson I share in this book is all about using time wisely, and that means making sure a variety of things are accomplished with and in that time. In the pages that follow, I will tell you stories of trial and error or pivots and of plain inexperience that helped me figure out better ways to utilize my time. Sometimes I needed to spend my time becoming schooled in the ways of doing business; other times I needed to spend my hours networking, finding mentors, and asking lots of questions. When I thought I didn't have time, I found some anyway in order to connect personally with customers, gathering intel that informed me on better ways to operate and manage my businesses. And a large amount of time was spent putting sweat equity in: doing the manual work that perhaps you'd hire employees to do, but at early stages, don't have the budget to do so. Marketing? Yes, I had to make time to learn that. Selling? That was an ever-present feature of usage of my valuable and limited time. When you are an entrepreneur, it isn't enough to say "Work smarter, not harder." It's both hard and smart all the day long. This book helps you gather your tools so you can utilize them and make the most of the precious time you have to reach your goals, find a work-and-life balance, and reach and exceed your expectations—the ones you've dreamed of all your life and the ones you didn't even know you had.

I remember when I was running Anytime Fitness (see Chapter 4) and I'd speak to guests who took out a one-day guest pass. When I asked them to enroll for the year and offered them significant discounts, many would respond with "I'd love to join, but I just don't have the time."

I'd say to them: "How important is your physical health to you? What kind of priority is it to stay fit? What role does keeping your weight down play in your life? How important is it to you to feel mentally and physically sharp? Might joining contribute to your avoiding the chances of becoming a prime heart attack (the number one killer of Americans ahead of cancer) victim? Is there something more important to you that takes precedence and prevents you from setting aside the time to join?" Some would join, and some would still say they didn't have enough time.

Make the time. Either join the fitness center and stay fit, or fail to attain your lifelong goals. What will it be?

Saying you want to be an entrepreneur and becoming one require you to ask yourself similar questions to the ones I asked to potential gym members. How important is your business or idea to you? What kind of priority is it to be in business or stay in it? What role does becoming a business owner or entrepreneur play in your life? How important is it to you to feel mentally and physically sharp? What would you be doing if you weren't running your own business or starting one?

And you have to love what you do. You can't be doing it because your mom and dad think it's a good idea, or your accountant does, or your spouse is steering you in that direction. It has to come from within, and you need to be passionate about it. It's all-in if you want to win. Half-hearted won't make you a success.

When I was starting out at Dunkin' Donuts and attending conferences and would speak to potential franchisees, I'd ask them what sparked their franchise interest. Their answers were telling. Some would say it's the best way to make a steady living, but they weren't really committed to running a franchise and figured it would be laborious work that would wear them down. "Too many hours and too many tasks," they'd say. I knew that those franchisees either wouldn't succeed or wouldn't last or both. They were going to be miserable in due time, and even if their franchises took off for a while, it would grind them down and sap their energy and spirit. There were just too many conflicts, too many disputations, battles, challenges, and obstacles, to keep them going in operating a restaurant franchise if they weren't, like me, totally committed to running a restaurant and making it fun while working hard.

For me, it's a joy to run a restaurant because I'm working for myself. Yes, I face problems/complaints every single day. Such as when the customer asks why the cashier got the order wrong or why the french fries were cold. Or wants to know where the general manager is to resolve an issue. And here are a couple more uncomfortable ones: Why did the customer write a negative review on Yelp that the fries were cold rather than coming to us to solve the problem? How did we manage to bounce back from the damaging hurricane? The list goes on and on and on.

And it doesn't matter what the business is. I write about restaurant franchises because I'm steeped in that business. But it cuts across any startup. Are you having to raise funding when you don't have sufficient capital? Looking for loans when banks don't want to offer money to the inexperienced? Finding friends, family, and business associates to invest in your business? Learning how to ask for money and where to get help? These are the topics and techniques I'll be covering through the rest of the chapters.

Not becoming overwhelmed, staying positive, and keeping your eye on the target are all just as crucial as the financial aspect. Combining the characteristics of resiliency with the financial know-how leads to getting a startup business off the ground.

But to me, every day is different. There are no duplicates. I'm never in a rut. Each day brings new challenges that I've never faced before, that keep me fresh and agile and responsive to solve the issue and move on from it, and please the customers and retain the employees. My day can change in a split second. I write a list of 12 things to do each day, and some days I cross off 8 of them—and sometimes none of them.

I will admit that I've wasted very little time. That's been one of my mantras, day in and day out: "Make the best of every moment."

And the satisfaction derived from running a restaurant chain is fulfilling. When the customer says to me, "Thanks for replacing the cold fries with the hot ones," it feels good. When the manager compliments me for interceding and solving the problem, it resonates for me.

Being poor as a child and teenager drove my work ethic. Most native-born people who are middle class or affluent often don't face the gritty struggles that poor people and immigrants encounter on a daily basis. Those struggles strengthen people. Yes, there were times starting out that I faced hardship and thought about giving up, as when every bank and credit union rejected my loan applications to buy the fitness center, one no after another. Or was it 10 noes or more after another? But I kept going. Nothing stopped me from achieving my goals.

All I kept saying to myself was that I needed an opportunity. And then I learned to tap the people who knew me the best: my friends and family and sometimes my colleagues. They believed in me, my character and efforts, and let their money show their faith in me and my business goals. I learned to sell myself. Here's my dream of opening a fitness center, or a doughnut franchise, or a smoothie chain. Here's why it will succeed, and here's why I have the know-how to make it work. Here's my detailed business plan, and here's how I will make your money back and can make it grow. "Come with me on this adventure to succeed in the restaurant business" was my underlying message.

I often had a vision of where I wanted to take the franchise or company a year from now, two years from now, and beyond. With Kountry Vodka (see Chapter 9), for example, we'd be selling 10,000 cases by the end of 2022. But by the end of 2023, with our new national distributor reaching every liquor store and bar in Illinois, I expect that number to grow to 100,000 cases. There are approximately 50,000 bars in Illinois, and we're hoping to reach the bulk of them.

The feeling to avoid, at all costs, is complacency. Once you think you're getting comfortable and have it made, that's the kiss of death that signals your fortunes will turn downward and diminish. Back when I was in the US Army at age 21 and on patrol in Baghdad, I remember my sergeant saying that when it gets quiet on the street, you'd better stay focused and on your toes. His point was that getting too complacent will relax you too much and prevent you from being prepared for the next attack. After the quietude comes the barrage, so you'd better be prepared.

The first year after I opened my first Dunkin', the revenue started to expand, and I thought I had it made. Then a tough winter followed with snowstorms, and revenue declined. And I wasn't prepared to cut costs and find ways to attract customers. I had gotten complacent after that first year and paid the price, and I vowed it would never happen again.

When I started out, I had two factors working against me: my age and my race. But I knew I could overcome my youth with devotion and hard work. And being Black to me wasn't a drawback or a limitation, but a calling to work that much harder to succeed. Moreover, I never looked for a government handout. I was dedicated to making it as a person first and letting my actions speak for themselves. By analogy, I always told myself that I wanted to learn how to fish, master it, and lure in the halibut or cod. I never wanted the government to give me the fish. Once I caught the fish, I conquered the challenge and could do it again. I wanted people to say: "Yonas earned it. He caught that fish."

But what I was able to do was to take advantage of the freedom that the USA offers its citizens. What I've learned is that the United States allows you to do whatever it is you want and whatever you set your mind to. With very few restrictions. If a guy like me who came here knowing two words, "yes" and "no," and learned "sorry" early on, could succeed, so could anyone else.

I learned to be fearless. If I survived during wartime, endured being shot and at first considered dead, I figured I could thrive in a normal, safer environment. If I followed my dreams, took the right steps, strategized, won people over, and did the job and did it well, I had the makings of a success.

I wasn't afraid of work—getting my hands dirty and working overtime. Every single day I pursued my dreams, the way gold seekers dig for gold, deeper and deeper, in an unwavering way. I tried to develop my own sense of charisma and grit, I sought out mentors, and I presumed that nothing was going to stop me from achieving my dreams. I focused on the task that had to be done, didn't let failures deter me, moved on from them, learned from them, and adopted a new strategy.

And when I had to close a Dunkin' during a flood, I didn't get bent out of shape or curse my fate. I solved the problem, kept things under control, and then moved on.

I envision a day in the not-too-distant future when I might be selling off some of my franchises and taking on new adventures. My next stage could be investing in real estate, or opening independent eateries, or who knows what.

But I won't be wasting my time. I'll be setting new goals and trying to achieve them every blessed minute of the day.

My pathway to success sets the route that nearly anyone can take. At the risk of simplifying a very complex story, starting at the bottom is necessary for most of us who don't come from families with great wealth. Starting as a dishwasher, a barista, a server in the restaurant business, a clerk in a small shop, or an executive assistant in a larger firm is a way to get your foot in the door and start learning. At the bottom rung of McDonald's and Burger King, where I started out, I could glean multitudes from the assistant manager and manager by asking questions and observing. Roll up your sleeves and dig into work, and others will respond to your curiosity. No matter what your job level is.

Start with a vision of where you want to be. You need to project into the future. For example, a salesperson in a local eyeglass store might say, "I can see myself as a manager of this eyeglass store, and the next step would be opening my own shop and specializing in fashion-first glasses." That vision will provide a road map of what steps you need to take to advance to your ultimate goal, and you can check them off one by one. For me, I saw all these Dunkin' Donuts stores, with many of them jam-packed with customers in the lobby. And that's what I envisioned for myself. Imagine if I could own one of them and find ways to keep it busy, and maybe own a second franchise, and then who knows how many more I could have? And for you, it takes imagining where you want to be in five years, and what it will take to achieve that goal and put it into action.

Success also means surmounting any roadblock you encounter along the way. And believe me, there will be plenty of roadblocks (as noted in the title of this Introduction) as you'll see I encountered in the ensuing chapters. It starts with not taking no for an answer. You'll get plenty of them, with people telling you "You can't do that" or "You don't have enough money" to do that, or perhaps, even, as I was told, I didn't come from the right background or the right side of the tracks. And then someone will say "Yes, it can be done," and you'll be taken aback for a minute, and then you'll progress to start achieving your goals, as I did.

And it doesn't matter what the business is. Car dealership? Warehouse? App? Online store? Food truck? You name it, and it will play out similarly.

Then there is what I call it the "flight-or-fight" conflict, where some people dig in and overcome and other people give up and flee. If you fight, you can win as I did, winning no matter how the odds were stacked against an immigrant with some community college credits making it in America.

When you're in these initial jams, your brain becomes overloaded, and it's easy, I will admit, to want to flee. That's the normal impulse. But just as you'll see it play out with me and my first Dunkin' Donuts, I dug in and managed to overcome my initial setbacks and haven't looked back since. Every business, whether a recycler of auto parts or a manufacturer, faces these obstacles. The gritty and resilient will win.

I am grateful to you for wanting to share in my journey with me. I will start at the beginning and always keep in mind your plight as an independent, creative, and ambitious entrepreneur and how my hard-earned lessons might translate to your life. It is my great hope that you will know the fulfillment of getting up in the morning and tackling the unknown and going to bed at night with the peace that you did your best that day, came to work and did your job and did it well, made a few customers happy, and put a few dollars in your pocket—and experience feeling the pride I feel today.

CHAPTER 1

A TOUGH CHILDHOOD PREPARED ME TO BECOME AN ENTREPRENEUR

It's the Grit That Helps Make You an Entrepreneur

My path—from immigrant to soldier to major franchise restaurant owner—winds through many roads, over many hurdles, and finally to a place in America we call success. My journey represents the ultimate immigrant success story.

It began when my parents fled civil war in Ethiopia and landed in a Sudanese refugee camp, where I was born, followed by our arrival in the United States when I was nine years old. I grew up poor in a public housing complex in Wheaton, Illinois, and enlisted in the US Army in response to the 9/11 World Trade Center bombings. In Iraq, I got shot with a rocket-propelled grenade, which earned me the Purple Heart. Ultimately, I became a partner in 47 restaurant franchises and owned two independent restaurants, a vodka company, and a butcher shop.

As Lin-Manuel Miranda wrote in *Hamilton*, "Immigrants— we get the job done." But my story also epitomizes the outsider's ability to overcome innumerable roadblocks to reach one's destination. I've often wondered: What exactly enabled me to endure and prosper? What drove me to overcome the traps, circumvent the obstructions, surmount the discrimination, and transcend my ragged upbringing? Like many immigrants, I mastered the necessary steps to become an entrepreneur. My outlook was "Obstacles be damned." And excessive hard work is only the starting point.

Having those day-to-day interactions with my managers, my fellow employees, and customers shaped my vision of success two decades later. I learned how to handle situations, how to take everything in stride, and how to treat customers along with my supervisors and colleagues. "Accountability," I call it. I learned that actions mattered, and how I treated people—everyone who came into those quick-service eateries—mattered and counted for something.

WHY ENTREPRENEURSHIP OFFERS YOU CONTROL OVER YOUR DESTINY

But make no mistake: It hasn't been easy. I've faced setbacks, discrimination, dashed hopes, poverty, and rejection, among other obstacles.

Even when I was living in poverty in the Sudanese refugee camp, my parents unknowingly set the stage for me to become an entrepreneur. When you grow up in a poor family, the prospect of becoming an entrepreneur holds a dream of financial freedom. You'd be able to help your family and, for that matter, friends and other people who require assistance. My parents always encouraged me to dream big—to reach for the stars.

Owning a business offers control over your own destiny. I may not have known this as a kid in that refugee camp, but by the time I got to high school in the States, I realized being part of an organization can mean you get laid off, and promotions often depend on one's college's insignia or ability to network, rather than merit alone. Owning a business is risky, but it gives you more control over your fate.

Once you own your business, it's hard work that separates the winners from the losers. The harder you work, the greater the odds you'll succeed. Building a thriving business depends on knowing how the system works and understanding the process. Overcoming obstacles plays a huge role in determining success.

But I also knew that there were several hurdles staring me in the face that could undermine my dreams. The primary one was that old-fashioned bugaboo: money. To become a successful business owner, you need to amass a certain amount of capital to get started even if you're bootstrapping and raising money on your own. It isn't easy to launch a business on a shoestring. I needed to save money and find the most strategic ways to raise capital if I was going to succeed.

DON'T SHRUG OFF YOUR ENTRY-LEVEL JOBS

Sure, when I was slinging cheeseburgers at McDonald's and Burger King, I didn't get much respect. Those entry-level jobs are about getting your foot in the door and gaining necessary experience. They're invaluable. If you watch and observe and ask questions, you'll learn the basics of how companies operate, what managers look for, and what it takes to please customers. These jobs are priceless and teach you the ins and outs of generating a business. That is, if you're paying attention.

Luckily for me, my part-time jobs as an adolescent set the stage for success. Starting at age 14, I worked at the service counter at my local McDonald's and then gravitated to a Burger King. The money was modest, at best, though it felt good to have some dollars in my pocket. These were entry-level jobs, but I learned the ways of the world there. Toiling at fast-food eateries taught me many skills that have stayed with me for a lifetime.

MASTER THE BASICS OF BEING A GOOD EMPLOYEE AND MOVE ON FROM THERE

You know that book *All I Really Need to Know I Learned in Kindergarten*. I learned the basics of entrepreneurial success in my entry-level jobs in the fast-food industry. For example, my managers drilled into me the idea that I had to show up on time every day. That might be considered the basics for almost anyone, but for adolescents, that could be a tough concept. Early on,

I showed up early and tried not to miss a day. And it has stayed with me 25 years later: Always show up on time, and come to work ready to perform.

But I learned a score of things starting out. For example, I learned how to communicate with adults, and the secrets of what worked with them and what didn't. Losing your temper came under the column of becoming ineffectual, so I kept a lid on this. For me, it wasn't difficult to restrain my behavior. I wanted to do what worked, impress my customers, and remain in sync with my management team, all skills that proved invaluable.

I could work no more than four hours a day after school because of work limits for teenagers, but on weekends, I could put in more hours. My parents made sure my schoolwork was done before I headed to my job. Having that extra money in my pocket enabled me to buy the latest pair of Nikes. But I was also learning what it took to succeed at work and in particular in the world of fast food. Those were hard-fought lessons that would resonate for years afterward.

AVOID TAKING THINGS PERSONALLY—IT SAVES A LOT OF HEARTACHE AND ANGUISH

I also learned not to take comments from managers or customers personally. "Clean up that mess, Yonas," was a fast-food manager's way of showing urgency. It meant "Do it now" before it worsens and a customer gets offended—not that I was doing a bad job.

One day, a lactose-intolerant customer to whom I served a coffee with milk exploded in anger and disgust—but she had actually forgotten to tell me she was lactose intolerant. While she screamed at me, I stayed calm and said, "I apologize. We'll fix it immediately and get it right." I deliberately avoided saying she had forgotten to tell me that she couldn't drink the milk because of a medical issue.

I knew if I engaged her, she'd be yelling at me, and then I'd likely scream back and amplify the pitch, and then my managers would intercede, and I'd be the loser. I apologized for something I didn't really do wrong to defuse the situation. These are the life-long lessons one learns at the service counter at McDonald's and Burger King.

Taking care of customers formed a legacy that would never leave me. It was one of the hallmarks of helping me succeed as an entrepreneur later in life.

What entrepreneurship ultimately meant to me could be summarized in one word: "opportunity." What would have been my fate if I had stayed in Africa, my childhood home? I'd most likely have ended up working in a sweatshop for pennies an hour, or herding sheep on the plains for a similar amount. Opportunities there were few or nonexistent.

I knew that America was brimming with possibilities. I recognized that even for someone like me, with only a high school diploma and a few years of community college, if I strategized, raised some money, took the initiative, and—excuse the cliché—worked hard, I could thrive. I could make something happen, even though I was Black, even though I learned English as a child and starting mastering it later in life, I didn't grow up in the United States, and didn't have the greatest vocabulary. Despite being raised mostly in poverty, I could make something of myself. I kept imagining what life could be.

When I was 19 years old and saw the World Trade Center attacked by America's enemies, I enlisted in the US Army. I wanted to give back to the country that gave me a chance to lead a free life. I was sent to Germany and Kuwait, and I served one tour of duty in Iraq.

On one expedition, while I was patrolling Iraq's perilous streets, I sensed a suspicious quiet. I could feel danger. When the enemy's tank arrived at an intersection, I heard the blast as a howitzer attacked it. I looked up almost instinctively and spotted two men with AK-47s. I heard the chief yell, "RPG (short for 'rocket-propelled grenade')."

The explosion knocked the M16 out of my hands. My breath was taken away, and when a fellow soldier checked my pulse and couldn't detect any, I was (as I later learned) pronounced dead—for about a minute. Then a medic found my pulse, hooked me up to an IV, stopped the bleeding, and calmed me down. In short, she saved my life.

I was immediately flown to the Army hospital in Germany for surgery. It was feared I'd lose considerable mobility, but I ended up losing only about 5 percent.

When I returned to the States, I was awarded a Purple Heart, which will always symbolize my duty to the country that offered me freedom and a chance to make something of myself. After my discharge from the Army, I focused on attaining my primary goal—owning a business.

In 2005, after serving in Iraq and recuperating in the hospital in Germany, I launched a painting-and-cleaning business.

WHAT MY FATHER'S FRANCHISING EXPERIENCE TAUGHT ME

Given my limited funds, I figured a painting-and-cleaning business would be the cheapest and most cost-effective route. As a

18-year-old, before I joined the Army, I was an apprentice painter at USA Painters; it's where I learned my painting skills. And my dad worked at Service Masters, a franchised cleaning service, so I learned some strategies from him, even at the tender age of 11 or 12.

My dad worked hard, cleaning offices and schools, and liked his franchising job. But I remember even when I was in junior high school his telling me that what the owner was paying him was a pittance compared with what the boss made. He bemoaned the fact that he didn't have a better education and didn't have enough money saved to open his own cleaning franchise. "Owning is where the money is at. Not the guy doing the cleaning," he'd say.

How much of that conversation unconsciously seeped into my brain early on? How much did it spur me on to start saving early and see if I could become the boss? I'm sure it played a subliminal role—at the least.

And the other thing that sunk in was that the owner of Service Masters was an immigrant named Mohammed. I remember my dad saying Mohammed worked hard to save his money. If it could happen to Mohammed, it could also happen to Yonas, I figured.

But my parents didn't want to hear about my opening a franchise back when I was in high school. To them, like most immigrant parents, it was about getting an education—going to school and earning degrees.

I learned one other invaluable lesson early from my dad when he was at the cleaning franchise. When on rare occasions, a customer complained about a specific job, he'd go after work to improve it. The customer is always right, he'd tell me.

The major difference between opening a franchised business and an independent one was franchisees could rely on the resources, name recognition, and established branding that had been built up over the years. Most people in the United States were familiar with Dunkin' Donuts, for example. But when you're opening an independent restaurant, the owner has to execute the menu planning, marketing, and branding on his or her own. And if you're starting an app, online business, or e-commerce site, it's all up to you as the founder to provide everything needed to get off the ground. Yes, franchises can be formulaic in one sense, but from a business startup vantage point, a lot of the groundwork is predone.

Even at that young age of 12 or so, I think the seed was planted that a franchise business was a way to build a long-lasting, lucrative career.

START SAVING MONEY EARLY—THE EARLIER THE BETTER—AND FORCED SAVINGS WORK

The other seed that was also planted early on was that it takes money and savings to launch a business. At a young age, my parents drilled into me that saving money was mandatory. It wasn't a suggestion. Even when I was making $200 and then $250 a week at McDonald's, I gave up my paycheck, and my mom would take out 10 or 15 percent (and later 20 percent) and put the money directly into a savings account at the bank. And $100 a month grew to be $1,200, and after two years, I had nearly $3,000, which back then felt sizable and made me feel special. It set the framework that eventually enabled me to have a portion of the down payment for my initial franchise.

Not everything in life is about money, but starting a business requires capital. That's just the way it is. That means putting money aside. It requires a mindset to save, not spend. Build for the future rather than indulging yourself for the moment. TV and social media ads encourage us to spend, spend, and spend. But if you want to open a restaurant franchise, you'd better start saving early. You won't have to outlay the entire franchise fee, and there are ways, even for neophytes like I was, to obtain funding, but you'll need to provide some capital of your own.

I saved about $10,000 from my years in the military and tapped that capital to buy supplies and business cards, and I was on my way to launching my painting-and-cleaning business. All I needed now were customers.

I started my business in Carol Stream, Illinois, one of Chicago's southwest suburbs. Compared with Wheaton, where I was raised, it wasn't affluent. But it contained mostly white people, with a sprinkling of Blacks and Mexicans, and so it was diverse, to a point.

I named my painting-and-cleaning business "Win Peace," which some might consider unusual. It sounded like some United Nations nonprofit organization out to change the world. But I named it so because I liked to win, and most people wanted to work and live in peace.

When I started going door-to-door to ask customers if they were interested in a new paint job or cleaning service, I'd get 100 noes for every client who said yes. That's no, no, no, no, no, no, no, and . . . you get the idea. The noes can wear you down. Having absorbed so much rejection, it would have been easy to think I wasn't qualified or skilled enough to provide that paint job for a client's living room or kitchen. I kept thinking that people were mistaken, and I was going to show them they were wrong.

Now, every entrepreneur faces rejections. Not just those like me, who are minority, are of Ethiopian heritage, spent time in a Sudanese refugee camp and, to most outsiders, comes across as a moderate-sized Black guy. The feedback I garnered was that I looked intimidating, and I had to tone that down by being affable, friendly, and open.

I've encountered so many misperceptions about immigrants, and those of African heritage in particular, it's baffling. I find most Americans generous, thoughtful, and respectful. As a country and a culture, America is special. Most Americans look out for their neighbors and feel pride in their neighborhoods and country. But let me tell you, there are plenty of uneducated or misinformed Americans who carry strange and fabricated, exaggerated ideas about what it means to be an immigrant in the US of A.

Through the course of my life in this country, I've had people say to me, "Oh, you're an immigrant. Did you come here on a raft illegally?" or "Did most people in Africa wear diapers?" Many didn't know that Africa is a continent, not a country. Many didn't know that most cities in Africa were modern, civilized, and bustling. When I told them that I flew here with my parents on a plane, and that we were legal immigrants and had green cards, they were stunned and stupefied.

Of course, when I asked them where their grandparents hailed from and they'd tell me Ireland or Germany or Russia, I'd think, "Your grandparents were immigrants, no different from me."

But walking door-to-door and hearing one no after another can wear a person down. When I was younger, rejection devastated me. "What is wrong with me?" I'd think. "Why aren't I good enough? Why don't the other kids like me?" As a kid, I didn't have the confidence in myself to understand the rejection.

As an adult, I didn't take rejection personally. In fact, the noes allowed me to move on and knock on the next door. It's resilience that pays off in business. Every no brought me one step closer to a yes. At least that's what I told myself, and that refrain kept me going.

Often, I thought I was being stereotyped when I tried to sell my painting-and-cleaning services. For example, I remember several times walking into a doctor's office, often encountering the executive assistant or office manager first. Most of the time, it was an elderly white woman who screened all salespeople. One of the things I always tried to do was to look as professional as possible to offset any preconceived notions. I'd wear a finely pressed pair of khakis and dress shirt to look as polished as possible and overcome any "Better keep my distance; he's from a ghetto" expectation.

Nonetheless, before I could open my mouth and offer my services, I'd often hear a "We're not interested." How exactly did she know the doctor wasn't interested in my services if I hadn't gotten a chance to explain what those services were?

One day, going into a doctor's office, I arrived at the same time as a paper supply salesperson. He was white and was offering paper supplies. She engaged him in conversation, asked some questions, and treated him with respect. The office manager heard him out, listened to his offer, and then asked me to step forward. As I began to talk, she cut me off and said, "We're not interested" in a record-shattering split second.

As I said earlier, each no inspired me to surge forward, overcome people's objections, and prove to them that my team and I could paint or clean their offices, apartments, or houses better than anyone else. You can say no, but I'm going to keep moving forward, knock on the next door, keep hustling and initiating, and eventually, succeed.

I discovered one saying that kept me energized: "Persistence beats resistance." I don't know where I first heard it or why it resonated for me, but I kept thinking nothing would keep me from succeeding. I can *outpersist* you. I didn't know or care if "outpersist" was a word. It became my byword, my how-to-beat-the-odds outlook. My mantra. My persistence can surmount your resistance. Watch this.

I also learned a considerable amount about using people's noes and coming up with solutions. When people would tell me there was no budget for a new paint job, I'd ask what they expected it would cost. Sometimes they'd reply that their last paint job cost $5,000, and they didn't have that kind of money now. "I could work with you on that," I'd reply. "What if we set a $3,000 fee, and you could look at my portfolio, see former paint jobs, and call my references?" That pitch won over scores of customers.

It was a fortuitous encounter with a friend at the gym that altered my sales pitch, helped solve the resistance problem, and set me on a path to success. I was disconsolate after a fruitless day knocking on doors. When I met Tim at the gym where we work out, he asked me what was wrong and had me describe my door-to-door pitch. I told him that I said my name is Yonas Hagos and asked if they needed a new paint job or cleaning service. Sounded straightforward enough to me. He scoffed at that and suggested that, instead, I tell them I was a Purple Heart combat veteran who served in Iraq. "Try that as a pitch and let me know how that goes," Tim suggested.

When I tried that strategy the next day, the world turned around for me. Instead of 100 noes for every yes, I got 7 yeses out of every 10 households. Eventually, I got so busy that I had to hire four other painters to join my team to keep up with the work. I started making good money and saving money (which would lead to financing my next venture).

People listened to me in ways they never had before. No longer was I just a 5-foot-10-inch, medium-sized, muscular Black guy looking for work. Now I was a medal-winning combat veteran. Even the ones who didn't need a paint job would say,

"Thank you for your service, young man." Suddenly I engendered respect rather than fear, dismissal, or the usual ho-hum rejection.

Despite adding my Purple Heart award to my pitch, there's a piece of me that prefers to keep it under the radar. Personally, I don't like calling attention to myself. In the Army, you're trained that everything is about the team, and everyone watches your back. Taking credit often doesn't seem right, but I'll admit it spurred my small business to new heights and differentiated me from other painters knocking on doors.

I also figured out new strategies to identify new clients. For example, the Jewel supermarkets were major players in Illinois, and at that time, many of them had an area where local businesses could leave their business cards. I put together a flyer with a take-off tab with my phone number. Every day, I'd circulate the flyer in three or four local Jewel supermarkets. The more strategic I became, the more business followed. It's the customers ultimately who keep the business alive. Meet their needs, and the business stands a good chance of succeeding. Slight them, and the odds of success are slim. The more I focused on what the customer wanted—good, quick, reliable service—the more I understood what made a restaurant thrive. Too many employees take the customers for granted or don't get clued in to their needs. It's all about the customers.

I also learned something about customer service, another key to success. I'd tell clients if they weren't happy with the work, they wouldn't have to pay. And I meant it. Few, if any, ever took me up on it. But my point was that we aimed to please and would do everything we could to paint a house or office to improve its appearance. If we didn't, or the customer thought we didn't, we'd redo the job. I learned to please the customer and exceed expectations. That led to a ton of referrals from friends, neighbors, and family, contributing to our success. Much of our business came from repeat customers, the key to most businesses' survival. That's true for Starbucks, CVS, Best Buy—or your local cleaner and painter.

The key was always satisfying the customer, just as my father taught me when I was in junior high school. We'd find out what people wanted and strived to deliver it.

But sometimes when you're an immigrant like me, it's very thorny and difficult gaining the trust of your client. My staff and I painted the house of one rather affluent woman. About every 10 minutes, she'd check on my two painters and me. Early on, I suggested to her that if she had any valuables, she should please move them to a safe place so we wouldn't interfere with them. Still, I surmised that she kept checking in on us to ensure that we weren't stealing anything. It was unnerving, but again, being an immigrant and Black, you come to expect some distrust.

How did my staff and I overcome her suspicions? First, I engaged her in conversation and encouraged her to get to know me. Once she heard that I was born in Africa, she seemed to calm down and trust us more. Maybe it just broke her preconceived notions of what guys are like who live in the ghetto.

On the way home, my two other painters asked me why that woman didn't trust us. I, of course, knew they were right to be upset. "Look, guys, the only thing we can do is do the job well. Impress people with our skill and do the job right." And they agreed.

What's the postscript to this story? Two months after we finished her job, I got a call from her daughter, who wanted to hire us. Guess we impressed her after all and secured her trust. "My mom said you did such a good job. Could you come over and give us a quote?" We could, and we did, and we were hired on the spot.

Another ingredient in the success of my painting business: Early on, I learned that price is key. If the going rate was $4,000 for painting a 1,000-square-foot house and I could undercut that by $1,000 or so, I could earn the assignment. Lowering the price meant generating more business. If we did that job right, it would lead to referrals and repeat work. Saving the clients money transcended the fact that I was an immigrant and from a minority group. I saved them money, and that was the bottom line.

When I hired people, I focused on reliability and trustworthiness—traits that were essential in the military. I wanted them to show integrity more than anything. If they were experienced, that helped, but I could always teach them how to paint. I couldn't teach them honesty.

Motivating them and providing incentives were other result-producing factors. If we had three jobs and we needed to complete them by Friday, I'd explain what they needed to do to accomplish that task. If they finished, I'd either give them a bonus or buy them lunch or dinner to demonstrate my satisfaction.

As alluded to above, my treatment of employees, in many ways, stemmed from what I learned in the military. Just as in the Army, when the sergeant said he'd never ask anything of us he wouldn't do himself, I followed that example. If my team got overwhelmed, I'd stir the paint or clean the toilets or do whatever it took to get the job done.

But based on my experience, I knew that loyalty was hard to foster. If another firm offered my workers a buck more an hour, they'd walk. No matter how much respect I showed them, money talked.

The chip on my shoulder also boosted my success. That chip developed when I was younger. I'd see white and affluent kids in school who curried favor with most of the teachers. I'd work hard and rarely get praised. I had to struggle to get out of ESL

(English as a second language) classes and had to repeat sixth grade. That felt humiliating, and I figured the other kids viewed me as stupid.

I always felt that as an immigrant, I had to work twice as hard as anyone else. As a person of color, I always felt at a disadvantage. We'd be questioned and scrutinized when other people were often embraced.

The main skill I learned as an immigrant who was constantly working for other people was to emphasize communication. My goal was to enable them to get to know me better and overcome any preconceived notions. I always tried to come across as the well-spoken professional. I learned to speak their language and constantly emphasized my team's professionalism.

It made me think back to my own education, which was fraught with roadblocks. It wasn't easy mastering a new language and culture. I remembered what happened in sixth grade, when I was held back. In some ways, repeating sixth grade was the best thing that ever happened to me. I mastered reading and improved my writing and extricated myself from ESL classes, which enabled me to mainstream and get into the regular public high school.

Back then, I felt angry when anyone taunted or derided me. At age 12 or so, that hurts; you haven't built up the defenses or the self-confidence to handle the ridicule. Now I tap the chip on my shoulder to vault ahead.

I realized more about the way the world works. It's not always what you do but whom you know. It's just the way of the world. The way I view things now is this: I'm the underdog, and I'm going to surprise you. Outwork you. Outhustle you. I'm going to win at running a painting business, or a fitness club, or a restaurant franchise. I don't get angry anymore. I work hard and show people how and why I can win.

In some ways, that chip on the shoulder helped propel me to greater heights. Since I grew up relatively poor, and my parents had limited education, I felt as if I had something to prove. It provided me with an edge. It pushed me on to always improving. Failure wasn't an option. "I had to succeed," I'd tell myself. And my growth in business proves that you don't have to born rich to succeed, but with the right attitude and perseverance, you too can make a success of your startup business, franchise or not.

There was another saying, besides the one about persistence, that reverberated for me: "The struggle is the success." You can't succeed without struggling. I came to embrace the struggle and learned to go with the flow.

Another thing I did when my business started becoming more successful was to save money. When I worked part-time at McDonald's from age 14 on (and as I first noted above), I'd hand my check over to my mother. Unbeknown to me, she saved half my check and invested it in a savings account at the credit union. By the time I was 16, the savings had proliferated.

LEARN TO AVOID OVERSPENDING— IT WILL PAY OFF IN THE END

Often, people who are doing well spend most—or, in some cases, all—their money. When the business is prospering, that's the time to save. At a certain point, I dreamed of owning a franchise, though I wasn't clear on what kind it would be. But I knew I might need to tap $300,000 or more to secure one (based on minimal Google research), so the more I saved, the more I positioned myself to be in the game. Frugality, along with putting my money to work and letting it compound, would help set me up for the future. So my $10,000 saving was growing gradually, and I kept adding to it when I started my cleaning business and then my fitness center franchise.

WHAT TRIGGERED MY FRANCHISING ITCH

I started getting the itch, at a rather young age, to explore franchising. Some of that emanated from my part-time jobs at the fast-food burger places and some from my father's tenure at the cleaning service. After I returned from the Army at age 22, I'd look at the Dunkin' Donuts franchise page. It said that you'd need some liquid cash to get started—you'd need about $300,000 to get it off the ground. I knew I didn't have that kind of money back then, but it lingered in my mind as something to aim for and save for.

What you learn from running a franchise is true for operating any business. The owner is like the leader of the band. He or she has to create a culture, set the rules, operate as a role model, and set the tone. And it doesn't matter if it's an online business, a small business, an e-commerce site, or a bodega.

THE OWNER IS THE LEADER OF THE BAND

The owner, the operator, the franchise leader, whatever you call him or her, of Smoothie King, Dunkin', Arby's, or Chicken Salad Chick, keeps everyone on the same page and creates the franchise's culture. Yes, the owner listens to the staff, but it's the leader who sets the tone and makes sure all the servers and bartenders, or other employees, are on the same page and create a unified approach.

Running the show is only half the battle. I still take a step back to feel how lucky I am to be an entrepreneur, to have the opportunity to build a business and succeed.

In that way, I also cultivate a sense of gratitude. Every time I begin to think the other guy is better off than I am, more privileged than I am, has an easier time than I do, I stop myself. I have a wife and two kids, and I'm making good money. I've adjusted to life in America, and as an immigrant, I have a good opportunity to succeed. I needed to struggle in order to succeed.

While I was still in the military and was stationed in Germany before I was shipped over to Iraq, I had a conversation with my friend Anthony Overstreet that resonated for years. Overstreet, as I called him, said to me, "So, Yonas, after your three years of service are up, if you come back alive, what do you expect to do? Are you going to college?"

Until then, no one had asked me that during my stay in the Army. It made me think. I had started community college, but the academic life wasn't for me. I thought for a second, and first replied, "Maybe I'll become a police officer or try to join the FBI." At that time, I thought you didn't need a college education to join either force (which has changed in the FBI and certain police departments).

Overstreet had gotten to know me and had a sense of me, and he felt that I wanted more from life than joining an organization.

"That's your dream?!" Overstreet replied, sounding stunned, picking up on the fact that I was grasping at straws. He added, "You don't have to go to college to achieve your dream. Bill Gates started Microsoft in his basement and garage and never completed his degree."

And then out of nowhere, almost unconsciously, I exclaimed, "I'd like to own my own business. That's my dream. Maybe start a restaurant franchise. I have the right background, having worked in fast-food places for almost five years before I joined the Army."

I knew that had been the case for a while. Influenced by my dad, I knew that owners got the major bulk of the profits, not the workers. It had been brewing in me for a while, but it was my Army buddy who got me to express it, for the first time, out loud.

Overstreet was the first person who ever asked if I had any dreams. It was inspiring to vocalize them. Just expressing them gave me hope they could happen.

In the African American community, the major ways to get noticed or famous or successful were to become an athlete, musician, or actor. People in those professions could transcend the limitations of growing up in tough neighborhoods, but most working-class minorities couldn't. Black neighborhoods offered few role models if you didn't have the gifts of Michael Jordan or Duke Ellington.

After that conversation with Overstreet, I'd daydream about owning a restaurant franchise. Of course, it was a way off, and I still had some hurdles to overcome. But just having the dream made me think I could make it happen. I didn't have to follow in the footsteps of many other Ethiopian immigrants and become a cabdriver or open an Ethiopian restaurant. I could become a business owner, an entrepreneur, and it all started with having the dream.

IT'S NOT WHERE YOU START; IT'S WHERE YOU FINISH

I once heard a song from the musical *Sweet Charity*, written by Cy Coleman, that said "It's not where you start; it's where you finish." I started at the bottom: cleaning up at fast-food eateries. But it doesn't matter what your first job is—whether you're a server, an assistant to a dry cleaner, or a fitness instructor—if you have the dream to move up, you can set the path to achieve it. It takes planning, and organization, and some money, and mostly personal conviction. Yes, I cleaned tables and took orders and fried the potatoes at a couple of global fast-food joints, and early on, I wasn't sure exactly where I was headed. But gradually things fell into place and jelled. And if it became true for me, it also could happen to you.

WHEN YOU START AT THE BOTTOM, YOU HAVE NO PLACE TO GO BUT UP

I think a considerable amount of my future success had to do with where I started: at rock bottom. I knew what it meant to be dirt poor and not know where my next meal was coming from. When I got my first fast-food jobs, I thought, how could I mess this up? If I put in my time and work hard, I can move on and up and out and thrive. I have a chance to make something of myself and my life, and there's no way I'm going to ruin it. After you've seen the worst of humanity and the struggle, you know you're going to strive to make everything pay off.

I wanted to work hard, get my fingernails dirty, work up a sweat, dig in, do the work, and avoid taking the easy way out. Now that I've put in my time and things are working out, I can enjoy the fruits of my labor.

I wasn't an insider. Other than being a member at a local fitness center, I didn't belong to any secret societies or entrepreneurs' clubs. Some call my path to success, "the school of hard knocks." But frankly, other than those door-to-door rejections, I wasn't battered and bruised. I wasn't a world-class networker, either, who thrust my business card into people's hands. Though several friends did help me with my sales pitch, and that did lead to a loan, I did it the immigrant's way: calling on my inner determination, doing the hard work and then some, and figuring out things on my own. If I can make it, so can you.

If there was one quality that made me successful, my "secret sauce," if you'll excuse my borrowing a term from my first employer, McDonald's, it was my persistence. I've seen so many people embark on a project or business, get close to success, stumble, and give up. They're like sprinters in a 100-yard dash who are out in front of the pack, look back, lose their focus, and fall. I never gave up hope that one business would lead to another and finally get me on my path to opening a restaurant franchise.

What did I learn in my part-time jobs in the fast-food business and my initial venture into the franchise business? I can break a few lessons down into steps I call the "Yonas way." Here's what I mastered and what I consider the key tips to becoming a successful entrepreneur.

— *Key Tips* —

FOR BECOMING A SUCCESSFUL ENTREPRENEUR

TIP #1
Before You Launch Your Business,
Learn to Be Totally and Wholeheartedly Self-Reliant

I've learned in life and on the job not to depend on anyone but yourself. Count on yourself first and foremost, and then look to others. In one of my first fast-food jobs, my manager asked me to clean the fryer. I had two tasks to do, so I asked a fellow worker if he could take one of the jobs to ease my load. He said he could. But the next day, the manager came to me in a huff, asking why the fryer hadn't been cleaned. My colleague got diverted and never started the task. I learned an important lesson that day: As much as you want to trust the other person, you can only depend on yourself. You have to know your strengths and limitations, what you can and cannot do, the core of the lesson being that you have to be accountable to yourself, and that sets up your opportunity to succeed.

TIP #2
When the Going Gets Tough, Stay Calm and Don't Get Bent out of Shape

It takes a certain personality to start a business, and that requires staying in control of your emotions. Getting bent out of shape quickly, being irritable or irascible, won't work. For me, working at a fast-food restaurant heightens my opportunities for face-to-face encounters with irate customers, who can, on occasion, scream, accuse, or rant at their server. "Why was that burger served rare when I asked for it well done?" "Where's the cheese I explicitly requested?" "Who stole my bacon?"

Remember, one of my first fast-food jobs was at Burger King, whose commercial promoted, "Have it your way," suggesting that the customers could build their own burger with whatever ingredients they desired.

But if you want to solve problems, take control, and defuse conflict, keep in mind one important lesson: Stay calm. The calmer I remained, the better able I was to solve the problem. If the customer was agitated and I responded with anger, frustration, and an equally hostile tone, the conflict worsened. Nothing was accomplished. Staying calm enabled me to extricate myself from the situation, calm my frustrated customer, and eventually resolve the situation.

TIP #3
Becoming an Entrepreneur Doesn't Mean You Don't Have a Boss

Many people in the nine-to-five corporate world (and that includes remote work) have a clearly defined boss who evaluates them, oversees their behavior, leads them and a team, and is part of the corporate structure. Many people turn to entrepreneurship and become like their former bosses, and that's fine. But everyone, including entrepreneurs, has a boss. And your key bosses are your customers. Without them, you don't have a business. You must listen to them, cater to them, adjust to them, please them, and respond to their changing needs. In some cases (if you're a franchisee, for example), the overriding franchise is also your boss, and you need to adapt to it, as well.

TIP #4
But Entrepreneurs Do Have Their Own Prerogatives

If you're working for a boss and the CEO acquires a company that tanks, employees may be demoted, shuffled into other positions, or fired to reduce costs. The CEO made the bad investment, and the employees, through no fault of their own, pay the price. Becoming an entrepreneur usually leads to financial freedom. The entrepreneur controls much of his or her fate, is responsible for making decisions, and has more say over his or her future. You're the driver, not the passenger. That is a liberating feeling that also comes with a series of pressures.

TIP #5
Taking Risks Is the Hallmark of Entrepreneurs

When I think back to my early days, I realize almost everything was filled with risk. I had asthma from early on, and that made breathing difficult. I was raised in a Sudanese refugee camp, where food was sparse and we were outsiders in that country. Everything was risky at best. Then my mom and we kids followed my dad to America, where everything was unfamiliar and complex. At age 19, I took a risk and joined the US Army. Every day on tour was frightening and put me in the line of fire. Taking risks was part of my DNA, so in many ways, starting a business when I returned to the States after my injury was a normal reaction.

TIP #6
But Keep Risks to a Minimum

If you're married with a child or two and a mortgage, leaving your job to start your own business can be dicey. Many decide to avoid the risk entirely. Understood. What if you open a franchise and the customers don't come? And you raise and borrow $300,000 to launch it and the business goes under? What will happen to your house and family? The fears proliferate—which is why many people play it safe. But there's a way to take the risk and remain intact. I call it "discipline," a principle we practiced in the military. Don't relinquish all your savings; hold onto some in case things go awry. If you make sound financial moves, you don't have to risk too much capital. You can open your business, and if things don't work out, get back into a career and earn steady money. You'll likely never regret giving it a chance, which could likely pay off.

TIP #7
Give Yourself an Exit Strategy

Lay out a plan, including having enough money to sustain your business for at least two years. That'll give you enough time to test it out and see whether it's viable. If it's not working, there's always the safer, corporate job that brings in steady money.

TIP #8
Failure Isn't an Option

Speaking for myself, failure wasn't an option. When I acquired my first Dunkin' franchise, I was waking up early, working 10 hours a day (or more), skipping lunch if I had to; nothing was going to get in my way of making it a success. Nothing. Everything I planned depended on that Dunkin' fast-food eatery thriving. Of course, success isn't guaranteed. But if I did everything in my power, performed due diligence, worked ceaselessly, solved problems, took care of my customers, and set up a structure that guaranteed return business, I'd succeed.

TIP #9
Keep Your Mind Sharp

I've learned that staying mentally sharp is one key to running a successful business. From the moment I enter one of my Smoothie King franchises, I'll look at the line of people waiting for their orders inside and also study the drive-through line. Do people look annoyed or frustrated, or are they being welcomed? Their faces will tell me whether my staff is taking care of business (literally and figuratively) or whether we need an intervention from the owner to spur them on to better customer service. I'm observant, watching, eyeing, concentrating for signs of customer reaction.

But it also involves doing your homework, studying the analytics, knowing when most of your customers are coming to your business. And it doesn't matter if it's a restaurant franchise, an app, an e-commerce site, a secondhand clothing store, or an ice-cream shop. Every business has an array of moving parts, so keeping in control of all of them is paramount. Staying one step ahead is one way to keep the revenue flowing.

TIP #10
The Key to It All: Pleasing Your Customer

Here's what I tell employees at all my franchises: Customers are the easiest people to please. My Dunkin' franchise in Normal, Illinois, gets so busy, we average 8,000 to 9,000 people a day. All they want is a hot cup of good coffee and a donut or breakfast sandwich, a warm greeting (by name if they're regulars), and timely service.

That's not too much to ask for, is it? As long as you give customers what they want, and do so efficiently, you can't go wrong. Most choose franchises like Dunkin' or Smoothie King because those places consistently deliver the same product, in a welcoming atmosphere.

TIP #11
Keep Expanding

I never stop looking to expand my business. I feel insatiable. I now own (and that number may have risen by the time you read this work) 47 franchises, including 32 Smoothie Kings, 9 Dunkin's, 2 Chicken Salad Chicks, 2 Rosati's Pizza, 1 Arby's, and 1 Nothing Bundt Cakes. And then add my own concepts, Silver Fox Bar and Grill, Dakotas Bar and Grill, Kendall Meat Company, and Kountry Vodka. And coming in 2024 we expect to open a Kaia Tapas and Beach Life for breakfast and burritos, and that makes close to 50 restaurants. One Dunkin' Donuts led to a second and third, and when the three were thriving, there was no stopping me. Read the next few chapters to see how one Dunkin' turned into almost 50 eateries . . . and counting.

TIP #12
Have Thick Skin

Every successful person—from Bill Gates, to Jeff Bezos, to Mark Cuban—gets overwhelmed by rejection and one no after another, just as I did going door-to-door with my painting-and-cleaning business before I adjusted my pitch. But what those noes do for you is to thicken your skin, make you tougher, so you don't take anything personally, expect the noes, and learn to move on from them. As I did through my first business. My skin got toughened and calloused from breathing in all those noes, and it made me a better person and more effective entrepreneur.

You're going to get beaten down, humiliated, scorned, and rejected. That all comes with the territory. But the winners pick themselves up and keep fighting and battling and clawing and bouncing back. That's what separates the winning entrepreneurs from those who need a safer, less risky environment.

But as hinted, it's the mental outlook that separates the successful entrepreneur from the forgotten ones. Which happens to be the subject of the next chapter.

CHAPTER 2

THE MIND OF AN ENTREPRENEUR

Succeeding No Matter What the Business Is

A s you already know by now, my success stemmed from owning multiple restaurant franchises. But what we're talking about and focusing on in this book far transcends owning one of those franchises—it involves operating any business.

Whether you want to own a shoe factory, or a shoe store, for that matter, or start an e-commerce site or app, or start with a food truck on a shoestring budget, or open a secondhand clothing store, it doesn't matter what the venture is. And it always entails knowing what the risks are and keeping them to a minimum. And as already noted in Chapter 1, it's for people who won't be deterred by failure. So no matter what the specifics of the business, these tips and lessons should enable you to overcome the key obstacles and devise solutions to nearly any conflict or problem that arises.

Everyone fails at something, including devising a business. Steve Jobs, the founder of Apple, had at one point been dismissed by Apple. Bill Gates had setbacks at Microsoft. And Elon Musk, once the world's wealthiest man (and still high up on the top 10 list) who founded and runs Tesla and owns Twitter, suffered setbacks. You're going to have setbacks. How you deal with them distinguishes the winning entrepreneurs from those cast aside.

Setbacks in my own background? I ended up having to close my painting-and-cleaning service and sell my fitness center before I embarked on owning franchises. Those setbacks were part of my path to success. Without them, and learning from them, I'm not sure if I would have been as successful as I've become.

Those failures helped me to understand my shortcomings. Not having a strong enough vision. Not building enough strategies to retain my customers. Not knowing how to retain staff. Not finding enough varied ways to keep my fitness customers over the long haul. I made mistakes, learned from them, and moved on. Every setback became a learning experience, something to conquer and push past.

I recently had a very rough time at work. At several of my franchises, things went wrong, both mechanically and staffwise, that made for an arduous day. It depleted me, to say the least. But the next morning, I woke up invigorated, ready to take on the world, solve these problems, and go on. It was my inner fortitude, the adrenalin that entrepreneurs thrive on, that enabled me to correct the miscues and drive forward.

One aspect of successful entrepreneurs I've noticed is that almost all of them are optimistic. You need positive energy to achieve your goals. If you think the business is going to fall apart and fail, it often becomes a self-fulfilling prophecy, and it will.

And your employees feed off your energy. If you're downcast and gloomy, it will have a detrimental effect on them. But if you're smiling, waltz through the door, and ask, for example, "Hey, Victor, what's up and how are you doing?" in an upbeat, buoyant tone, your employees feel your burst of energy and want to emulate you and convey that to their customers. It's infectious.

Entrepreneurs need to be emotionally tough, withstand criticism, which can come at you from all sorts of directions, and constantly find ways to problem-solve. Nowadays snarky comments can come your way in person or on Yelp or Trip Advisor. I was recently in Florida, sitting on a rock, observing a flock of seagulls. They flew away without finding food—that is, all but one. One remained by itself, watching, and then saw some fish in the water and pounced. The patient seagull solved the problem, and that's how entrepreneurs have to be all the time: problem solvers.

And owners need to be adaptive. Who could envision a pandemic that would change customer habits and lead to almost everyone staying in? Or a supply chain snafu that would make obtaining raw materials difficult and expensive? Or earthquakes, floods, and fires in an intensity we've never seen before? Every day for an operator varies, despite having set routines. The adaptive ones thrive.

And yes, franchisees have it easier in the sense that they enter a proven concept, with protocols that have proved successful.

This book is aimed at people who have a vision for themselves about starting something that is bigger than themselves. And it often springs from a personal passion, as has been stated.

This makes me think of what in my past turned me into an entrepreneur. One of my first and fondest memories was sitting on my beloved grandmother's lap, when we still lived in the Sudanese refugee camp. I was as young as four, maybe five, but I still remember the things she said to my mother about me back then.

"That boy Yonas of yours is going places," she told my mom.

She had watched me cut up cardboard and turn it into make-believe cars. I'd also separate wood and transform it into toy cars. Sometimes I'd take paper and mold it into make-believe shops and restaurants; anything I could do to keep me occupied and forget where I was.

The hut we lived in when we were in the refugee camp was built of straw and mud and managed to hold off the rain, but we were living with just the bare necessities. Luxuries there were nonexistent. Putting food on the table was the goal of every day.

Sometimes I'd go barefoot, and sometimes my dad would have enough money to buy me, my two brothers, and my sister sandals. Our family of six often slept in one part of the floor together, crammed in.

"I'm going to grow up and buy you a house, Grandma," I'd tell her.

I believe that what she saw in me that stood out was my imagination. Nothing could restrain or deter my imagination. Despite our decrepit living conditions, I could dream about another life, far away, that would make me happy.

But life was tough in the refugee camp; make no mistake about it. My siblings, including my brothers Solomon and Amanuel and sister Azeba (this was before my sister Rahel was born), and I didn't have any toys, so we made do with what we had: milk crates and boxes. We tried to make them look like cars and go for a ride and make believe we were on a highway somewhere. We played cops and robbers with make-believe guns. We let our imaginations run wild.

We had no electricity at night, no radio, and no TV except for one 19-inch set in a nearby tent that ran on a generator. Every now and then my mom would take us there to get a glimpse of TV, where we saw a world beyond our limited scope.

At night, we had lanterns or candles with wicks that offered minimal lighting. But that was it. Sometimes when the full moon was out, it would light up the skies, and we could play outside. But that only happened once a month.

And there were some terrifying moments. One night when I was about five, I was alone with my mother while my father was away trying to earn money. Even though our mud hut was behind a strong, barricaded gate to keep outsiders and thieves away, that night Sudanese soldiers with AK-47 rifles entered our lodging, looking for contraband.

Sudan was a Muslim country, which outlawed liquor, and to earn extra money to buy food my mom had an illegal moonshine operation hidden away, where she made liquor and sold it. If it was found, she could be imprisoned and separated from our family, or shot.

The soldiers didn't know for sure she had moonshine, but they did know that immigrants had to make some money to survive and that was one of the easiest routes to take. Hence, they were suspicious. The savvy soldier knew that my mom wouldn't divulge her hiding spot, but often the kids, when rewarded with candy, would unknowingly spill the beans and point it out.

This night a soldier offered me some candy and exclaimed, "I know you're a good boy. And I know your mom is hiding something. Tell me, where is it exactly?"

I put my head down, embarrassed for a moment. Though I was shy at that age, I knew enough to reply, "No, sir, nothing here." Frustrated, the squad of soldiers departed, but before leaving, one sent a terrifying reminder to my mom: "We'll be back. We know you're hiding something." We were saved that day, at least for the moment.

But the soldiers always loomed as a menacing presence. Instead of trying to protect us, they were there to ensure that we didn't get out of line. They were looking for refugees who were breaking rules, pushing the envelope, and trying to exploit regulations. From an early age, you learned at the refugee camp to lie low, not call attention to yourself, and not get into the path of soldiers out to entrap people.

Danger lurked in every corner of the refugee camp. There were groups of thieves who would steal from people's huts anything they could get their hands on, including money, jewelry, food, valuables, liquor (which, as just noted, was illegal)—anything. In the camps, there was no 911 emergency number to call to make sure the thieves didn't get away. You were on your own to safeguard your property and yourself.

We had several cousins nearby who would sometimes act as deterrents and stand guard or be on alert, which people in the camp knew about. We were lucky enough not to be targeted, but it took constant alertness to ensure our safety.

Because you never knew where danger lurked, the area we played in was fenced off from our neighbors. Though most of our neighbors were good people, there were some that were dangerous, rotten people, and my mom didn't want to take any chances that we'd fall victim to any of them. We always had to be under adult supervision if we were out playing our games, despite being walled off. The message was clear: It's a dangerous world out there beyond the family, and you have to play it safe or pay a price. As kids, we didn't exactly know what price we would have to pay, but we didn't want to find out what it was.

The only time I ever left the fenced-in area was when my devoted uncle took me on a walk to a candy shop to buy me a bottle of Pepsi or a candy bar. To me, back then, those were wonderful treats. They were tasty, soothing, and sugary.

Most days involved drudgery. We lived in a confined space where, as I said, danger always lurked, and other than playing, there was no place to go and little to do. The only things that broke through the boredom were holidays like Christmas and New Year's Eve. They were special days in the Ethiopian culture, and my mom would prepare dinner and bake. Cousins would come over, and we'd chat and laugh, and for at least a day, it felt special, almost festive.

Since I was the oldest, my two brothers, Solomon and Amanuel, would bombard me with questions and often flummox me. We saw a movie once on TV where someone was flying an airplane. The next day, the questions started multiplying from my younger brothers:

"Yonas, how do the pilots fly the planes?" Solomon asked me.

"How exactly does a plane get the momentum to fly?" queried Amanuel.

It was one question after another, and frankly I didn't have an answer for any of them. My inability to respond to their inquiries made me feel stupid and weak.

"Leave me alone," I'd say most of the time. Sometimes I'd concoct some totally fictitious answer just to get them off my back. But that often would trigger other inquiries that I also didn't know the answer to. When you're the older brother, you just can't win, it seemed to me.

Each day my mom would walk me and my two brothers and sister to school, to a different corner of the refugee camp. I had to carry my chair with me because the school was too threadbare to supply chairs. The school had a dirt floor, with few books and no amenities, and we were there Monday through Friday.

We were poor, but so was everyone else at the refugee camp, so we didn't stand out. In fact, my dad had a bus and transported passengers into town. His work managed to put food on our table, on a steady basis. Most days it was three meals a day, although sometimes it was two. But one thing stood out: We never went hungry, and living in a refugee camp, that was quite an accomplishment.

School was vicious. If you yelled out an answer, the teacher could come over and slap your knuckles with a stick, bloodying them. Teachers treated students as if they were animals, out of control. Their goal was to keep students in line, but that's no way to handle a child. It was cruel and unnecessary punishment and stultified one's sense of curiosity and learning.

I felt stuck in school, trapped like an animal caged in the corner. I wanted to scream and break loose and try something new, embark on my own path. I wanted to be free.

And yet I had some major outlets: my mind and my imagination. Despite living in so much danger, and feeling confined, and worrying about being robbed or mugged, my thoughts would go in all sorts of directions. I'd escape into my own world, thinking about flying away and being free.

I'd dream about America. From seeing some Hollywood movies, I imagined that there were flying cars in the United States and spaceships galore. (This was before the time of Jeff Bezos and Richard Branson building their own.) I fantasized about flying in one of those cars and escaping the horizon into one of the spaceships and winding up on Mars or Pluto. Maybe it symbolized feeling stuck in this refugee camp, where the options were few and there was minimal freedom of any kind.

In the United States there were places like Toys R Us, a store with unlimited (at least that's how it appeared to me) toys where you could walk in and, if you had some money, leave with a

Superman outfit, or a Batman cape, or a spaceship. What better place could there be for a kid to ponder when trapped in a refugee camp?

That camp also gave me my first taste of entrepreneurship—in an elementary way. To earn money and buy necessities, as I explained above, my mom started a moonshine business. She produced the liquor and sold it. Sometimes she'd complain that she made too much product one day, had to discard it, and lost some money. But often there'd be five or six customers, and I would help serve it. She could have given up, but she didn't. And I think that was one of my first lessons of owning a business, that you had to persevere, just as my mom did.

Had we remained in the camp and not immigrated to the United States, I'd likely be dead by now. That's not even pessimistic; it's just realistic. Migrants in camps have been hit by famine and disease and their lifespan is short. The media has so much to cover that it virtually ignores migrants' life in places far from the United States like the Sudan.

But strangely, life in the camps taught me things back then that I was unaware of. It trained me to be self-reliant, to depend on myself, and that strengthened me. What are entrepreneurs but people who build a business on their own and make it successful? You rely on your team, but most of all you fall back on your own resourcefulness. That quality took shape in the refugee camp. And though it was grueling there, and in many ways, dangerous and frightening, it built my character. My self-reliance started there.

It taught me that outside of my mom and dad, you had better depend on yourself. No one is going to bail you out. No one is going to save you. It's all about your own confidence to get the job done. (Then the military reinforced that attitude a little more than 10 years later.)

Back at home, my parents were also having problems. My dad had been married previously and had four children who were aged from 12 to 17, the oldest one being about 8 years older than I was. My dad seemed morose much of the time, trapped supporting too many children, not making enough money and knowing he had to do something to create a better life for all his offspring.

His relationship with my mom soured. He began hitting her. He was unhappy and took it out on her, and everyone in the household suffered.

Despite the uneasiness and tension, I still loved my dad and wanted to spend time with him. Maybe because I was the oldest, he took me many places with him, which made me feel special. He'd take me to movies at the refugee camp, and I'd see what life was like in America. That gave me hope that one day we could live a freer life than being boxed in all the time, not having enough food, or clothes, or electricity.

And then in the late 1980s, in search of a better life for all of us, my dad immigrated to the United States, settling in Houston, where he secured a job in the oil business. He'd send money back to us—at least until that job dried up.

I think I started to learn something about persistence from him. He had many mouths to feed, but he managed to find a way to create a new life for himself and for his family.

Then, at the suggestion of a friend, he moved to the Chicago area, about 45 minutes south, in Carol Stream, Illinois. There he worked as a cab driver.

My father sent us pictures of what his life was like in the States. When we saw a photo of the television he owned, we became extremely excited. To us, he was leading a life of luxury. He slept on a bed, and some of the apartment complexes had swimming pools. I'd imagine what my life would be like, swimming in a pool. "It doesn't get any better than that," I thought to myself.

After living in the States for over a year and a half, Dad returned to Sudan to announce some news. "You're all coming to live in the United States," he told us. "The US is a land of opportunity. You'll be able to get an education. You'll be able to become whatever you want to be." We were all ecstatic and dreamed of our new lives there.

Before we could get our visas, though, we'd have to live with my mom's cousin in Khartoum, the capital of Sudan, where we were interrogated by people in the US State Department. They wanted to make sure that we weren't terrorists, that we were interested in a better life, and that we were who we said we were.

Our trip to Khartoum was the first time in all my nine years that I had seen or encountered a white person. No one in the refugee camp, where I had spent my entire life, was white. I found it scary at first because the State Department administrator looked so different from us. We were raised to feel that white people were higher than us and better than us and wielded power over us, but this woman was so respectful.

She gave us chocolate to ease our fears. She asked me if my mom really was my mother, and the same about my dad.

When she asked me what I wanted to do if I immigrated to the States, I told her, "I want to go swimming in a pool. That's my dream." Luckily, she laughed.

When my dad, who had by then returned to the States, called to ask how the meeting at the embassy went, my mom said, very upset, "Yonas may have screwed up. He told her he wants to go swimming in a pool. That's why we're moving to the US." But then she calmed down and laughed and said, "Everything went well." Finally the green card and visa came through, and we planned our flight to the United States.

On his next-to-last trip to Sudan, before the final trip when he returned to Sudan to get us, my dad sat me down to lay out what we were doing. "You're going to be living in the US where you're going to have to work hard if you want to succeed," he told me.

"I could try to go to school myself, but I'm too old," he continued. "So I'm doing this for you and your siblings. You're going to be going to school to get an education so you can make something of yourself. The sky's the limit."

"I don't want you to waste your life," he concluded. "You have to make the best of it."

Despite the nerves that fitting into a new country triggered for me and the fact that I only knew two words of English— "yes" and "no"—my overall outlook on making the move was one of total optimism and unbridled expectation. In Sudan, if you had a TV, you were considered wealthy. From watching TV and movies, it seemed like everyone in the United States—or nearly everyone—had electricity and a TV. In America, you could become somebody.

The day we left the Sudan was the first time I had ever been in an airport or seen a plane up close. Everything was new, and the planes looked enormous. I'd be flying in the air and arriving in a new country! It felt like it was going to be a magical ride to America, and, in fact, it was.

After a layover in Italy, we flew to New York City and finally to O'Hare Airport, to our final destination in Chicago. It was a three-day trip all told.

In Chicago, a score of relatives who had also made their way there welcomed us. I felt as if my life was just beginning. Driving home from the airport at night, I felt the difference: There were no bumps on the road; everything was paved. Back in Sudan, the roads were filled with potholes that could ruin your car. But in America, the streets are paved with smooth roads.

When we were driving to our new town in Illinois, I started seeing things that I had never seen before.

I pointed to one thing in particular that I didn't recognize. "Mom, what is that?" I asked.

"It's grass, Yonas," she replied. I had never seen grass before. It was so green, like a lime. It looked so fresh and inviting, but I never saw anything like it in Sudan.

I couldn't wait until the morning to see other new things. What could be next? Everything new awaited me. For a moment, I felt free instead of being held captive in a refugee camp in confined quarters.

In our new apartment there were only two bedrooms, so the four of us kids (my sister Rahel wasn't born until 1994 so that's why there were four of us) slept in two single beds, two to a bed. But to me, it was all the room in the world.

And there was something else that I didn't recognize. "Dad," I asked, "what is this thing on the bed that feels so soft?"

"It's a pillow, Yonas; it's there to lay your head on. It helps you to sleep." In America, I thought to myself, we sleep on pillows that help you fall asleep faster! And I had never seen a mattress before. It too felt soft. I felt as if I were sleeping on air.

In the morning, I saw a contraption in the kitchen that I didn't recognize, either. It was a microwave oven, which my parents told me you could use to heat up food quickly, like milk or coffee, or if your tea got cold, or leftovers of any kind.

America had so many wonderful things I had never seen before—pillows, mattresses, microwave ovens. "What would tomorrow bring?" I wondered.

The next day we went shopping at a Jewel supermarket. I had never seen anything like this large grocery store. When my dad got to the entrance, the doors miraculously opened before him automatically. We had no idea how it operated. It was magical and some kind of modern-day miracle to us. It took us several trips to accept that these doors were letting us through without having to push a button manually.

But one problem, for me and my siblings, was that everyone was talking in English, and we didn't speak the language. As I noted before, the only words that I knew were "yes" and "no." Everything else sounded like gibberish. How was I going to adjust to a world where I couldn't speak the language and I only knew two words? That wasn't going to get me very far. "I have to learn English, and learn it fast," I thought to myself.

Whenever I expressed annoyance at my not understanding more English, my dad would get irritated. "You'd better start figuring it out," he exclaimed.

We started to read books in English for the first time. And then we started to watch the shows *Barney and Friends* and *Sesame Street* and the Muppets, and our vocabulary started to build. When I first watched the Muppets, I thought they were real animals. I didn't know they were puppets. I thought they were real animals that talked, like a dog or cat that speaks. First, doors that flung open automatically, and then, animals that talked! Because so much was new to me, and so much was overwhelming, and we came from a place that didn't have television, I didn't know what to make of things. Finally, on second viewing, I learned the Muppets were puppets and started getting a better sense of my new enhanced, modern world.

As soon as we could, we started playing outside and met the children around the neighborhood. Kids being kids, one of the first things we learned was how to curse. I'm not going to repeat those words to you, and my mom and dad weren't beaming at our newfound list of profanities, but it added to my repertoire of yeses and noes.

As a kid, you just pick up new words every day. And learning new words and expanding your vocabulary seemed natural. Each day my language skills would grow. Even though my parents still spoke their native tongue in the apartment, they started adapting and speaking English so my brothers, sister, and I could absorb the language.

When I started school in the fifth grade, I was placed in English as a Second Language classes, which fit my skills. Though I was making incremental progress, I had to repeat sixth grade, which initially felt like a setback. "I'm not stupid," I thought to myself. "I can learn." But in many ways, it was the best educational thing that ever happened to me. It helped me gain confidence and strengthened my language skills, and finally I entered regular classes and got off the ESL track.

One day in seventh grade, one of my fellow students said to me, "You have an accent. Are you Jamaican?" He started laughing and obviously was mocking me, but I thought to myself, do I have an accent? I didn't think I did. When I returned home, I asked my younger sister if we had accents.

She laughed and said, "We all do. We're from someplace else. Though your friend was wrong thinking it was Jamaican."

That was a revelation to me. I started becoming much more cognizant of my own accent, tried to pronounce words more carefully, and did everything I could to minimize or eliminate it. Of course, that fellow student was being cruel and nasty, but that's what kids who are 11 years old do to one another. Ironically, it had a beneficial effect, as I really concentrated on speaking English properly and correctly, without any accent, Jamaican or not.

When I was in middle school, money was tight, and my parents would shop for shoes for us at Payless, where footwear was cheaper. But the affluent kids in school wore name brands like Nike and Adidas, and that defined them. Other kids would make fun of us for wearing nameless brands.

But when I started working part-time at McDonald's and then Burger King, everything changed, because I started having money in my pockets. I started purchasing Nike sneakers with the money I earned. Walking into school with my new Nikes on made me feel like king of the hill. I felt special. No more Payless no-names for me anymore. In fact, I felt downright cool. And when you're 14 years old, there's no better feeling than that.

The only issue that arose because of my new wardrobe was that my younger brothers, Solomon and Amanuel, would "borrow" my new Nikes without asking me. And that would concern me. I loved my brothers, but couldn't they at least ask—and not just take?!

In other ways, my brothers taught me how to be responsible for other people. These were skills that helped me when I enlisted in the US Army since you operate as a team and are trained to look out for everyone. If one person in my platoon crossed the line, we were all held responsible. These were traits that also enabled me to do well once my restaurant franchises were up and running.

Living in that two-bedroom apartment with my two brothers and sister and parents was, as expected, cramped. Because I was the oldest, I would be blamed for anything that went wrong. I was supposed to protect my three younger siblings from any wrongdoing. And if they took one step over the line, it would be me, Yonas, who was blamed, not them. If Solomon and Amanuel got into trouble in school, my mom wanted to know why I didn't prevent it or protect them.

Even back then, even when I was growing up and making mistakes and fighting for direction, I wanted to own a business.

My goal was simple: I wanted to be rich. Being rich would grant me the freedom that I desired more than anything else. If you worked for other people, you were beholden to them and had to follow their rules, and you could be dismissed for no reason at all.

At that point, I wasn't sure what direction I was headed. Would I become a music producer? A rapper? Own my own clothing line? Be a movie producer? It didn't matter to me as long as I could call the shots and generate as much money as possible.

WHAT DROVE ME TO LAUNCH MY OWN BUSINESS

I wanted to control my own destiny. If a CEO made a bad decision, everyone at the firm paid for his or her mistakes. I yearned to have 99.9 percent control of the business. I would be responsible, for better or for worse, but dependent on my own hard work and efforts. Some things, like the pandemic, you can't control, but running a business, I could oversee and steer just about everything.

And that made me wonder what successful entrepreneurs have in common. No matter what the business. Some of it revolves around natural talents that can't always be taught, like inner fortitude, where there are no Zoom classes to master it. But some of it entails taking one's natural talent and having coaches and mentors shape your talents. Lebron James is a naturally gifted basketball player, but even he had coaches along the way that refined his skills.

As you read on, you're going to find ways to start your business. And overcome whatever obstacles stand in your way. When people get to know me, they ask me how I started, where did I find the money. I usually reply that it's all about your network, finding the friends and families and colleagues who know you, trust you, and believe in you. Few of us have enough cash to invest in our business on our own.

The biggest hurdle to launching a business is people themselves. People who hold themselves back, yield to their fears, only believe in themselves half-heartedly, and don't give themselves the chance to follow their dreams. Read on.

Key Tips

FOR THINKING LIKE AN ENTREPRENEUR

TIP #1
Consider Every Failure a Learning Opportunity

It is inevitable that businesses will undergo setbacks. Customers will reject you. They'll speak up and complain about service (see Yelp or Trip Advisor for any restaurant if you don't believe me). Even a behemoth like Coca-Cola failed when it jiggered with its secret formula and introduced the New Coke, which most consumers rejected. But every failure provides new information, of where you went awry, and signals to you that another strategy is warranted. I remember reading about Burger King's introducing its new french fries with much fewer calories. Only they were tasteless, consumers rejected them, and they brought back their higher calories, salty fries. They listened to their consumer and reverted back. So listen, accept the failure, create a new strategy, and move on.

TIP #2
The Boss Sets the Tone

As the owner or entrepreneur in charge, you set the tone for the office, the small business, the techie repair shop, the food truck, the Smoothie King, whatever the business is. If you're upbeat and enthusiastic, people will follow your lead. If you respect people all the time, give constructive criticism rather than berate, belittle, or humiliate people, your staff will respond rather than shut down. You set the tone of what is acceptable in the business, and what isn't. So treating everyone with respect, from the dishwasher to the sous chef to the server, is predominant. And that leads to treating the customer with respect. Whatever demons you have, once you're the owner or boss, it is time to unload and extricate them from your behavior, or you'll feel the ramifications in a very short time.

TIP #3
Use Your Humble Beginnings
to Create Your Success Story

Sure I've met plenty of successful people who took over their business from their parents. Or who attended Ivy League schools, often following in the footsteps of their parents, or moving from an elite private school. And good for them. But for some of us who graduated from the school of hard knocks, starting out in entry-level part-time jobs can serve as a pathway to success. It's where you learn how to control your response, turn a negative encounter with a customer into a positive one, developing empathy to see things from the boss's viewpoint or the customer's, or a teammate's, for that matter. So starting out in entry-level jobs isn't sexy and often doesn't pay well, but it grounds a future entrepreneur from learning the ins and outs of every possible encounter.

TIP #4
Maintain That Sense of Wonderment

As an immigrant to the United States coming from a third-world country, much of what I experienced in my new country had never happened to me before. I hadn't seen grass, as basic as that was, and that elicited a sense of wonder in me. How beautiful was that green grass, finely cut, and how aromatic did it smell? Or passing by that automatic door at the grocery store? Did it know I was coming? That sense of wonderment has stayed with me about nearly everything I've accomplished in life and helped propel me to success. How exhilarating was it to see that long line snake around the block at the first Dunkin' Donuts we opened? And keep that line coming day after day? Or open a second brand? Or teach an employee to make the perfect smoothie? Or have a customer thank me for my employee who greets them every day? How magical is that? Maintaining that sense of wonder fuels success.

TIP #5
It's All About Gaining Control

Corporate employees can reap huge salaries and bonuses and be very happy with their job and their compensation. But for those of us who want to become entrepreneurs, taking orders, fitting into the bureaucracy, and playing politics to get ahead don't make us happy or satisfied. Entrepreneurs like to initiate, introduce new ideas, invent strategies, and call the shots. Yes, it can be considered a risky life, and there are no guarantees and often no pensions. But that sense of self-reliance and self-satisfaction transcend everything for people like me, and many of you who are reading this book. So take the initiative, launch the business, make all the right moves, and the rewards will come.

CHAPTER 3

GETTING THE BUSINESS OFF THE GROUND

*Keep Your Financial Risks
to a Minimum and Do Your Homework*

Some would-be entrepreneurs start very early having the itch to launch their own business from a rather young age. Others catch the itch at a later age, when, often feeling too tied down by their corporate handcuffs, they develop a yen or passion to venture off on their own. There's no right age to start a business; it varies from person to person.

For me, it all started back at the tender age of five years old when I was at that Sudanese refugee camp. The civil war was ending, and my dad was vying for a job in the United States and started talking to us about what life would be like in America. "It's a land of opportunity," he'd tell us, where you could become whatever you want: a businessperson or a doctor or a teacher. All you need is some education and some drive. I was convinced that great things would happen if we could come to America.

In some way, the younger you are when you launch your business, the better off you are, though clearly it can happen at any point. But for everyone who starts a business—a recycling business, a new app, a food truck, a dating service—it doesn't matter what the specialty is—the owner will undergo some sacrifice. That's the given in entrepreneurship.

If you're in your thirties and beyond, and you are making $100,000 or more at a steady job, with four weeks of vacation, a health plan, and an IRA, all those benefits will vanish once you start your own business. Your cushion will be lost. As will extensive time spent with your family. Sacrifice will rule your life; that's what it takes to get a business off the ground.

For me, it was 12 hours a day, sometimes even 14 or 16 hours a day. No vacations. And even in my free time, I was thinking about my business. There was no respite. I dreamed about solutions to customer problems. It doesn't matter if the business is a restaurant, independent bookstore, or e-commerce store on Etsy; it will take over and consume your life. That's what it takes to launch a business and make it successful.

If you're younger, in your twenties and thirties, you'll have more energy and stamina, and that will make getting the business off the ground easier. Of course, you can start it when you're in your forties or later; it's just tougher to muster up the required energy to keep it going.

If you fail when you're younger, it's easier to bounce back, straighten out your finances, and get yourself back off the ground.

Many people have asked me, "When's the best time to launch your own business?," and that's an impossible question to answer. It plays out differently with each person, and there are no definitive responses. For many people, there's a feeling inside that they *must* start their business. It's like a novelist that has a story to tell that can't be squelched. That driving idea of the environmentally sound recycling business, or the dating app for a new audience, must be released—it can't be stopped. When the passion is driving you, and you have the finances in place, it's likely the ripe time to start.

Some people start their business on the side, while still maintaining their full-time job, to lessen the risk, and that is a strategic way to get it off the ground.

Most people do their initial research on the internet, figuring out what they must do to start their recycling business, how much money they will need. But I recommend that early on you start networking in the industry you want to pursue. Knowing what the hurdles are, the major roadblocks, before you launch your business will alleviate many woes and conflicts along the way.

As well, getting to know as many people within the industry as possible is crucial before you embark on starting your own business. The connections I made helped me to raise money and know what I was in for before I opened my first Dunkin' Donuts, and your connections will do the same for you no matter what the industry.

Then, of course, you will need to raise money right out of the starting blocks of your new venture. My advice always is to start with family and friends who know and trust you, and where they'll recognize you won't be committing fraud in taking their money or scamming them, but investing in a venture to grow. It's always toughest the first time, because you have no track record of success. Once you do, investors will find you.

When I started my business in the early 2000s, the internet was operating but wasn't at the center of our universe, the way it is today. Nowadays websites such as GoFundMe (www.gofundme.com) can be another way to bootstrap a business to get it off the ground.

When I started my painting-and-cleaning business, I started with a minimum of $500 before investing about $5,000 that paid for my used van, a paint sprayer, cleaning equipment, a vacuum, and paintbrushes. Now, $5,000 to me was an acceptable sum that I had saved, but some people would call it starting a business on a shoestring or pennies, compared with the hundreds of thousands it can cost to open a small fast-casual eatery in Manhattan, for example.

There's one other quality that you'll need to become an entrepreneur. You'll need to be a risk-taker who has the guts, the chutzpah, as it's called in many circles, the gusto, to launch it. If you want to play it safe, the corporate world often—but not always, with layoffs always a possibility—offers some semblance of security for some people. But opening a business is for people who want to plunge into the deep water.

Starting out with an entry-level job in the business you want to pursue is another way to minimize risk. You'll learn the ins and out, whether you're in a startup position or you're a manager.

Be aware, though, that the odds are stacked against you—and I mean this only in a cautionary way, not a negative or pessimistic way. In my industry, the National Restaurant Association, the largest organization of restaurant owners, reported that over 30 percent of new restaurants fail in a rather short period. So the odds are 1 in 3 that any new eatery will shutter in due time. Of course, that can also mean that 70 percent stay open for an extended period, and that's a good thing, but you need to be a risk-taker.

One other piece of advice: Focus on the task at hand, and don't spend excessive time worrying about things you can't control. Worry about today, and tomorrow will come. Take each day one at a time to do whatever it is you need to do, to keep advancing your business, but you can't do it all in one day. It won't happen overnight. One small step at a time. "Focus on the mission at hand," is what I tell myself.

Without risk, there's minimal reward. And if your new business succeeds and expands, you will reap the rewards, as I have.

Entrepreneurship isn't for everyone. You must be a hard worker, dedicated to the task, and have an ability to not give up and to accept one no after the other. Failure is always a possibility, and can be a temporary step, to learn from, reorganize, and start all over again.

In my own life, starting a business felt risky, but not nearly as dangerous as walking on patrol in Iraq, where you could get shot by a rocket-propelled grenade, as I did. The biggest risk you ultimately face as an entrepreneur is financial. If you're using your own money, you could lose that. If you're tapping a friend's or family member's capital, you run the risk of losing it and damaging your reputation with people you care for.

———— *Key Tips* ————

TO GET YOUR BUSINESS OFF THE GROUND

TIP #1

If Possible, Keep Your Investment to a Minimum

If you can limit your exposure to losing money, as I did when I launched my painting-and-cleaning business for $5,000, you can lessen that anxiety. I viewed my first business as this wondrous opportunity. And being able to keep my initial financial investment to a minimum, I had little to lose and a lot to gain.

TIP #2

Knowing What to Invest Is Key

Once I saw that my painting-and-cleaning business was generating a clientele, I decided to invest some more money to make it easier to run. I was able to turn my $500 into a $5,000 investment by buying a used van and some equipment. The idea, as I said above, was to keep my financial investment to a minimum, so if things took a turn for the worse and I couldn't keep generating consistent customers, the loss would be manageable and wouldn't set me back too much.

TIP #3

Overcome the Early Rejections

I'll admit that, at the beginning, getting one no after another made me feel humiliated. I thought of giving up the first time a potential client uttered a no, and the second time I got a no, and then the third time . . . you get the idea. But my desire to succeed kept me going. I pushed on despite feeling shamed by the quick dismissals. Strangely, however, every no strengthened me. As I've said, my skin got tougher, my mind became more resilient, and I was dedicated to making this business thrive.

Someone I know used to say that every no is one step closer to a yes, because normally you have to knock on 25 doors or so in the painting-and-cleaning business, and this is also true for many other businesses, before you land a job. So every no didn't set me back, but just helped me to keep going. Staying positive makes your life easier than being riddled by questions of why people are rejecting you.

TIP #4
Stay Disciplined

In the military I learned to focus on the task at hand—not to project into the future, or to be overly concerned about what could go wrong—and to get the job done. That advice has proved useful on the job. Avoid getting bent out of shape or being overcome by worry. How do we speed up the drive-through line? Focus on problem-solving that conflict, and then move on to the next issue. Stay disciplined. One problem at a time. Just as in the military, where you focus on your objectives and don't get sidetracked by some setbacks.

TIP #5
Acquire Expertise Beyond the Books

Not everyone can graduate from Harvard Business School where you master the ins and outs of running a business. I didn't. Nonetheless, I acquired the know-how and savviness the old-fashioned ways: through on-the-job training. Even when I was a budding fast-food employee, the lowest person on the corporate totem pole at McDonald's or Burger King, I started asking my boss questions. I asked the owner where he amassed the money to start the business. I asked the manager, who also wasn't a Harvard Business School alumnus, how he mastered the skills to oversee a team of young, multicultural staff members. He started out as a fast-food employee and asked questions. "The same thing you're doing, kid," he replied. "Ask away." And most managers and owners like to see self-initiative in their employees; it helps them to stand out.

TIP #6
Hire the Right Staff

I'll admit it. When I first launched my painting-and-cleaning business, I knew little about hiring staff and read a book about how to conduct an interview to start it all off. I asked questions, such as, "What is your track record of getting to work on time?" "Why is it important for you to get to work on time?" "What do you know about meeting customer needs?"

What I've learned through the years is that, increasingly, new recruits train for these upcoming interviews. They watch videos, learn about what to say and what not to say, and often sound as if they've been scripted by the internet, or maybe artificial intelligence. So asking these general questions, as I did at the outset, doesn't accomplish much.

Now I've learned to ask questions that reveal the person's character, and that aren't covered, for the most part, by internet preparation. "What is your one-year plan and five-year plan for yourself?" I'll ask now. And those answers are more telling.

One applicant, interviewing for a manager's job, revealed to me that his one-year plan was to leave this job and open up a franchise and that he had been saving money to do so. Unbeknown to him, he revealed too much and wasn't hired. I wasn't looking for a one-year fix, but a manager who was dedicated to the job for the long haul.

I also ask about people's favorite hobbies. Many of the younger men will respond with basketball, or video games, and that's fine. But there was one who divulged that he liked to smoke pot off the job much of the time, and he wasn't hired. Pot in small doses, I suppose, may be acceptable and legal these days in many places, but frequent use isn't good for the demanding concentration required on the job.

Note that these questions will work for an internet job, or a manager's job at a software company or recycling company, or a marketer's job for a new dating app and will transcend franchised eateries.

But many fast-food employees are what I call "hoppers," and that means they move from one restaurant chain to the next, going where the hourly fee is better or the opportunity is appealing, and that's fine, too.

Hence, I'm essentially looking to dissect people's character. Are they self-reliant? Can they be team players? Will they take feedback from their manager? Will they arrive early and stay late? Can they problem-solve? Those are the attributes that work best on the job at my franchises, and for the most part, at your business, too.

TIP #7
Keep Your Spending Down and Make Frugality Your Lifestyle

If starting a business on a frugal budget is necessary, then reducing your own spending is part of the equation. You never know what can go wrong with your business that will press your need to inject more funding into the business. Nowadays, weather events can ruin the finances of a business. I've faced, for example, tornadoes and floods at many of my fast-food cateries.

Though I use a business credit card, in addition to my personal one, I try not to overspend and am dedicated to avoiding credit card debt, which is like a poison that worsens all the time. Debt creates more debt, and the deeper enmeshed you get, the tougher it is to extricate yourself. Keep your debt to a minimum. Use your credit card judiciously and wisely. Avoid debt if you can. Living below your means heightens the chance of having enough funding to tackle any mishap that is likely to occur.

CHAPTER 4

KEYS TO LAUNCHING AND RUNNING A FRANCHISE

Obtain the Right Funding and Minimize Your Financial Risks

started the painting-and-cleaning business first with myself and two employees and gradually doubled that to having four to six employees. Though the business had been growing and was generating steady income, when the recession struck in 2008, business at the company started to fade. Most people were seeing their 40l(k) portfolios shrink significantly, and people were forced to cut back on buying nonessential products and services, among them home improvements like painting. The paint job targeted for this year could wait another year. Or two. And so could the cleaning.

And yet I had come a long way. I had proved to myself that I could make a business work, attract new customers, develop a pitch (thanks to the feedback from my friend) that was effective, manage a staff, and keep a business afloat. It would spur me on to my next venture, which turned out to be another stop along the way before I finally discovered my niche.

Despite everything I learned about not taking no for an answer and believing that the no today would turn into a yes tomorrow, when the noes started multiplying, I could see my business fading.

As I thought about closing the business, I came to a realization about its imminent failure: Every time something falls apart, I've come to see it as a learning experience. I'm going to make mistakes, but I'm committed to not repeating them. Fail, learn from the failure, and move on.

But in 2009 the recession was at its zenith, everyone was running scared, and no one wanted to take on additional costs. When the business dried up and my constant flow of customers responding to my pitch as a Purple Heart recipient faded and then disappeared, there was nothing to do but close.

I needed steady work. I secured a job in Joliet, Illinois, at a chemical plant owned by the Koch brothers, Charles and David, two kingmakers who owned several energy, oil, and gas companies. The plant offered bonuses, paid my bills, and enabled me to start thinking about my next venture. I started working at the warehouse, packing products; then I started driving a forklift and then got promoted to operations at a water waste treatment plant. The chemical company paid well, and within the two years that I worked there, I was earning six figures, eventually to the point where I was making $124,000 a year, enabling me to save money.

But I was still working for other people, who controlled my fate. My goal was to work for myself, become an entrepreneur, so I could steer my own ship and be in charge of my own fate.

My dream was to own a franchise. Franchises are a proven formula. "Why reinvent the wheel?" I kept saying to myself. Franchise owners know their brand has a track record of success. You have a manual to train and guide you and help you understand the operation. If you run it right, you make money. The skills I learned in my initial business would help me to operate a franchise.

Much of that dream stemmed from my youth. As I mentioned earlier, starting at age 14, I worked part-time at McDonald's. Some people might criticize McDonald's, but as I see it, McDonald's developed a successful formula and kept it in place. What's wrong with that? The company offered customers—often poor and working class, but from all backgrounds (trust me, affluent people dine there, too)—tasty, inexpensive meals. And that was true for Burger King, where I also toiled as an adolescent.

When I started working at Burger King, it was for AmeriKing, a large franchisee that operated more than 400 Burger Kings. It was like working in an automobile plant because everything functioned like clockwork, little time was wasted, everyone had a specific job, and customers got what they wanted.

AmeriKing inspired me. The people there knew how to get the job done, run the business, and please customers. If only, I dreamed, I could reach their level. It is what some people call "aspirational." Could I, an Ethiopian immigrant by way of a Sudanese refugee camp, having settled in suburban Illinois, operate a slickly run franchise?

And then I found my mentor in the most unexpected of places. I was working full-time at that Koch brothers' chemical plant that I referred to earlier and needed a physical release to have some balance in my life, and that meant working out. Whenever I felt stressed out, I'd jump into my car, no matter what the time, and head to the gym to lift weights, run around a track, or do push-ups, which is what I did at the 24-hour, 7-day-a-week Anytime Fitness Center.

Ron Greenleaf was the franchise owner of that Anytime Fitness, and he and I became friendly. He had a full-time job as an executive at Bridgestone Tire, where he spent most of his time. Therefore, his wife helped run the club.

When I shared with him my entrepreneurial and franchise goals, he started encouraging me. "You could do what I do," he'd say. "You could continue working at the petroleum plant, earn a steady paycheck, and launch a franchise. All you need to do is come up with the startup cash to become a franchisee."

For me, a fitness center was the perfect business for my franchise career. Working out was my passion. Some of this may have stemmed from my military background: Working out and staying fit were crucial to being disciplined, staying alive, and maintaining my stamina. And yes, I would need to come up with the startup cash—and do and learn a lot more than that as I launched and operated my first franchise. What did I do and learn? Read on!

—————— *Key Tips* ——————

FOR LAUNCHING AND OPERATING YOUR OWN FRANCHISE

TIP #1
Learn How to Raise the Capital to Launch a Franchise

Ron Greenleaf emphasized that one of the keys to being selected as a franchisee was obtaining the necessary capital. Now that was daunting. Yes, I had saved money, but I hadn't accumulated enough to pay the full franchising fee based on what I had read on the franchise's page. So how could I access that capital with just a full-time job and accomplish my dream of owning a franchise? But Greenleaf kept reiterating it's viable.

What I came to realize from talking to him, talking to others, and doing my homework and research, was that as an initial franchise owner, you don't have to have the $225,000 or $300,000 saved to finance the business. What you need to do, for example, is to save about a third of the amount, or $100,000, and then find investors. If you haven't amassed that much capital on your own, I advise that you tap the people who know and trust you the most who are family, friends, and colleagues who have extra money and are looking to invest it and gain a return. Then search out SBA (Small Business Administration) loans (we'll explore that in more detail below), which are loans taken out from a bank, either national or local, that are guaranteed by the government. If you don't have a track record or sufficient collateral, most banks are not going to lend you money without the SBA interceding.

If you can find five friends or family members who have $15,000 or $20,000 each to invest, you've amassed from $75,000 to $100,000 in capital and are well on your way to putting a down payment on a typical restaurant franchise. And it doesn't have to be a restaurant franchise, because hair salon franchises, fitness centers, ice-cream shops, fix-it and repair shops, Pilates studios, florists, you name the business, can start from $150,000 to $200,000 to open.

Remember, though, those fees are only the starting point. Sometimes you have to buy the land or construct the franchise, and then you have to buy the equipment in some cases and pay salaries. And with most franchises, about 11 percent of your weekly receipts are turned over to the franchiser to pay for royalties and marketing, which cuts into your bottom line.

TIP #2
Limit Your Own Financial Exposure

When I told Ron Greenleaf that I was interested in acquiring an Anytime Fitness Center franchise, he checked my credit rating and saw that I was a good candidate for a loan. Eventually he directed me to one of Anytime's major equipment suppliers, which would grant me $120,000 in financing that would cement my becoming an Anytime Fitness franchisee. The supplier saw it as a win-win as it would make money off the loan and secure me as a steady customer.

For me, it meant limiting my financial exposure. Yes, I was taking out a loan, but I knew if I could increase the membership, I could repay the loan and make it lucrative on my end.

So that's why I invested about $100,000 of my own funds that I had saved from my cleaning-and-painting business to acquire the Anytime Fitness franchise. You have to have some skin in the game to buy a franchise, but keeping it to a minimum will lower your risk in the long run.

The problem with obtaining capital when you're starting out is, most often, banks will reject you. Without a successful track record, they consider you too risky. Then when you become a success and don't need them anymore, they start calling you incessantly to encourage you to take out a loan!

An acquaintance of mine who was starting a venture once had a problem obtaining a loan because she didn't have a track record. So she raised money through friends, and when her business became successful, loan officers kept calling to offer her money. "When I needed them, they weren't there for me, and when I became successful and didn't need them anymore, they kept knocking on my door," she said.

TIP#3
Obtain an SBA Loan

The SBA's specific role in the government is to create jobs via small-business creations. Small businesses employ 61.7 million workers in the United States, or 46.4 percent of all US employees. The SBA works with banks, no matter whether local, regional, or national, to make it possible to obtain loans by guaranteeing those loans to lessen the risk.

Robert Steiner, director of the Illinois District US Small Business Administration in Chicago, explains that the banks use several criteria to determine whether to grant the loan. These include:

1. The applicant's credit score. He suggests you make sure to boost your credit scores as much as possible before applying.

2. All of an applicant's financial information, including income and savings. This information should be compiled, written down, and squared away before applying. You'll need to fill out a personal financial sheet showing your income, your assets, and your debts. The form will be used to assess whether you're able to repay a loan.

3. Demonstrating management experience, of operations and/or staff, preferably in the industry you're focused on, or at least another one, and that includes being partners in a business, managing an office, and leading and guiding other people, so it can play out in several ways.

Steiner also reminds applicants that the banks make the loan decisions, and the SBA guarantees them. Therefore, an applicant has to first connect with a bank, often the local one that handles the person's accounts, or larger ones such as JPMorgan Chase.

"Once the bank does the underwriting, it sends the info to the SBA for financial review," he says. Applicants who visit the SBA website can also explore Lender Match, which helps people communicate directly with a series of lenders.

Steiner also emphasizes that anyone, whether an immigrant or minority or both, like me, is eligible for an SBA loan. "The criteria lenders use regarding SBA loans are agnostic to your background," he explains. The decision is based on "your business plan, your credit score, your collateral position, repayment ability. All are objective."

I received my SBA loan under special military veteran status. But Steiner notes that "most banks' criteria for lending to veterans doesn't stray far from the same ones for other applicants." He does point out one major difference: "Most of the fees are waived for veterans."

Steiner also explains that the loan amount can vary widely, starting as low as $500 and rising to maximum loans of $5 million. Many start at $50,000.

My experience was during the 2008–2009 recession, when banks weren't offering small-business loans—especially to neophytes like me whose only business experience was a small painting-and-cleaning firm. I knew my chances were slim to none.

I had no fitness experience as an operator, and lenders weren't giving out money because times were so hard. But when I contacted the SBA, my past shined a positive light on my character. The SBA told me I qualified for a military veteran's program. Apparently I'd been linked with an SBA-approved bank that issued these loans. All I had to do was fill out several forms and submit my tax records and military veteran certificates. It was painstaking but worth it when my loan of nearly $100,000 was granted. The loan was issued by JPMorgan Chase.

When I finally accumulated the $300,000 to launch the fitness franchise, the funding stemmed from three sources: my own $100,000 investment, $100,000 from the bank via the SBA loan, and $100,000 from the equipment supplier. The $100,000 of my own money that I invested was a huge percentage of my savings at that time, but I felt it was necessary.

At times, I could feel the pressure. What if we were to lose my $100,000 investment? I also owed the bank money for the SBA loan, which added more pressure. Pressure on top of pressure. How would losing the money affect my life? If it ever came to that, I could declare bankruptcy, face the music, and move on. But the better of me felt, deep down, this is America. This is the place where dreams come true. I won't let myself fail. I will do everything in my power—and more—to make this work.

In 2009, I raised the capital, took out the necessary loans, and became an Anytime Fitness franchisee. Who could have expected when we flew into the United States from Sudan or when I was wounded on an Iraqi street, that one day in the not too distant future, this immigrant would become a success? Though I was used to working hard in both the Army and my painting-and-cleaning business, I didn't know how hard I would have to work as a new franchisee with a full-time job.

TIP #4
Develop a Business Plan

Robert Steiner says that if you're a startup entrepreneur launching a business, you invariably "don't have much of a history." Therefore, what lenders and underwriters want to see is your business plan—how you're going to grow and, most important, how you're going to repay your loan.

A business plan serves as a road map of what you're going to do to execute your business in a step-by-step format. It lays out what the business will specialize in, what the target market is, what the business's competitive edge is that will differentiate it from its competitors, and what it will take to open the store or business. This will require doing research on similar businesses close by and devising ways to define and differentiate the business from its closest adversaries. The business plan can be adjusted as the business environment alters, but still it sets a course for the entrepreneur and gives investors a chance to evaluate the business's overall scope.

Banks, loans officers, and the SBA review the plan. It can play a significant role in helping lenders to invest in the business. It describes how the owner will turn the business into a success.

Startup entrepreneurs are expected to lay out the kind of revenue they expect to generate in years one, two, and three, specifying how they will reach those numbers. That will enable lenders to make comparisons to startup businesses that exist already in the same sphere.

"You don't want to be overly positive and say 'we're going to make $5 million a year' without a basis for justifying those financial projections," Steiner says.

It is really the bankers—large banks like JPMorgan Chase, Wells Fargo, Citigroup, Bank of America—and a host of independent and community banks that make the decisions about the SBA loans. But the SBA serves to minimize the risk because it guarantees 50 to 90 percent of the loan in the case of default.

Steiner also recommends that neophyte entrepreneurs arrange free consultations with the Small Business Development Center to help them draft their business plans and applications. And there are several nonprofit centers that can also help. Two of these are the Women's Business Development Center, based in Chicago, and a nationwide program, Community Navigators, whose goal is to foster entrepreneurship in underserved communities.

TIP #5
Learn from Mentors

Most often, mentors are people in the industry that you're pursuing who are experienced, know more than you, and are willing to communicate with you on the best steps to take and those to avoid. These mentors impart knowledge, savvy, and experience to you, but for the relationship to flourish, it must be reciprocal. In a certain way, the mentee must offer something in return such as curiosity, inquisitiveness, and/or enthusiasm, which provide some benefit to the mentor. Keep in mind, therefore, that the mentor must reap some benefit as well.

Since I was pursing the fitness industry, I tracked down the owners of Anytime Fitness Centers that were far enough away not to be seen as competitors to the one I was purchasing. I'd say something like, "My name is Yonas Hagos, and I'm about to buy an Anytime Fitness Center, and I'd like to pick your brain. Can I come over so we can talk for a half hour?" Most were open, looking at it as if we were playing for the same team, but some declined, which is their prerogative.

I shadowed the owner of a nearby fitness center for about two hours a day and got to ask plenty of questions and see how he signed contracts and explained the positives of joining a fitness center. I do think the training could have been better structured to teach the most germane skills.

Some offered me invaluable tips on how they marketed their fitness center, attracted new guests, retained them, and provided some benefits to new members.

And another critical factor I learned was that location played a critical role in a fitness center's success, just as it does in a restaurant franchise thriving. If the fitness center was close to a major thoroughfare, that helped. If it was situated in a well-lit shopping center, that could help attract people who didn't want to join a club that they wouldn't want to visit after dark. Location, location, location played a major role. Looking into the future, when I opened up a Dunkin' franchise, the prevailing wisdom was that it should be positioned "in their way and on their way," and that would attract the most customers. This society believes in instant gratification, and no one wants to wait long or drive too far. Hence, location is critical.

TIP #6
Curtail Your Operating Expenses

Once I had raised enough money and opened an Anytime Fitness franchise, I learned quickly, and through necessity, about operations—and specifically about how to cut corners. Our revenue at the beginning wasn't meeting expectations, so I had to look for ways to reduce the budget. For example, my business plan had me hiring more instructors to strengthen our experience and clients' satisfaction. But I wasn't able to do that. In fact, it took me more than a year of building up business before I could hire more fitness instructors.

It also took me a while to figure out that the instructors were one of the key tools to boosting membership. If they were talented trainers, established strong rapport with members, and knew how to emphasize the club's strengths, our membership grew. If they only went through the motions and didn't show enthusiasm or form relationships, we were stagnant in membership.

My then-girlfriend Kristie (now wife) became the sales manager, which became another key factor in determining our survival and growth. She had previously been an administrative assistant in a doctor's office, and though she's bright and industrious, sales wasn't her natural forte. So she had to learn on the job. Finally as membership grew, I was able to hire a real, trained sales manager.

I took an ad out and hired Nicole as sales manager. When you can't do a number one job in sales, it's time to pursue a pro. Nicole knew how to introduce herself to people, take guests on tours, show the fitness center's strengths, and explain the costs and what members got for their money, and she knew how to close a deal. She had pizzazz, she had charisma, and she had the sales skills to boost our membership. So starting with 120 members, after a year and a half, we had more than quadrupled membership to 500. Her efforts were pivotal.

Another aspect of keeping costs down was negotiating as many fees as I could. One thing I learned from owning a fitness center was that nearly all prices were negotiable. When I was buying fitness equipment, I discovered that the sales staff started by quoting one price of say $8,000 for a stationary bicycle. When I responded that I couldn't afford that fee but could pay $6,000, or 25 percent less, we negotiated and agreed on $6,500. So a little give-and-take saved me $1,500 per bicycle.

TIP #7
Determine the Breakeven Point

Once you acquire the franchise or business, it's time to think about the crucial number: the breakeven point. Add your rent to your employee cost, supplies, and equipment fees, and you determine that you need, for example, $10,000 revenue weekly to break even. Anything beyond that is profit. Once you see that you can make the breakeven point and become profitable, then you're on to something.

At first, margins were tight, and profits were hard to come by, and it made for an anxious beginning. By analyzing my costs, loans, rent, payroll, and marketing, I had figured out that I needed to generate about $20,000 a week in cash flow to pay my bills. My goal was to get my operating costs as low as possible. The lower they were, the easier to pay my bills and turn a profit. I finally lowered my operating costs to $8,000 a week, and there were still times I had to dig into savings to pay my bills. One or two months I took out credit card loans to pay my bills.

But I started with 120 members, and then through reaching out to new members, creating a welcoming atmosphere, and emphasizing Anytime Fitness's strength over its competitors, we built up membership (as noted above) to 500 a month, and money started to flow.

TIP #8
Learn to Overcome Preconceived Notions

The first thing I had to overcome as the new proprietor of Anytime Fitness was the reaction of the members when I introduced myself as the owner. Several people put out their hands to shake mine and asked, "What National Basketball Association team do you play for?" Guess they assumed only a professional basketball player could afford to own a fitness club. Given my relative youthful age at 27 years old, several members asked, "What NBA team does your dad play for?" Sometimes I kidded with them and replied, "No, you got that wrong. I'm a defenseman for the Blackhawks," the Chicago hockey team with few if any African Americans. I found their reaction prejudicial, or at the least, presumptuous, but I clenched my teeth and forged ahead. I was determined not to let other people's perceptions affect me.

Other times, a fitness member would see me in the lobby and ask, "Where's the owner?" I'd reply, "I'm the owner. How can I help you?" I'd see the shock and dismay on their faces, since Black men running the show was not their expectation. "Are you kidding me?" their faces would say. But in nearly every case, as we got to know each other, we'd overcome the preconceived stereotype and form a relationship.

One member who had signed a yearlong contract came to see me to extricate herself from it after three months. I don't think she ever thought I was really the owner, just someone standing in for the real one. But she was irate that she couldn't break the contract. She threatened to contact corporate. When I told her that was fine with me, she became belligerent. When corporate told her these leases couldn't be terminated, she seemed to calm down finally after considerable growling.

When I told a friend how exasperating it was to deal with these members' lack of acceptance of me as the owner, he offered some sage advice: "Learn to ignore it. Don't sweat the small stuff. Life's too short. Don't take any of their comments personally." Gradually, I put these principles into practice, and it was a freeing feeling.

Sometimes, Black members would support me. They'd see a white member giving me grief, and they'd come up to me afterward and say, "I like the way you stood your ground." "Hang in there and stay strong." When you're Black, a minority, or an immigrant (in my case all three), you become inured to this kind of ignorance. My skin is thicker than an armadillo's, I'd think.

Other times, Black members would tell me that seeing me in charge empowered, energized, and encouraged them to pursue their own dreams. Now, that made me feel special.

TIP #9
It's All About the Customer Service

Whether it was the fitness center, the painting-and-cleaning business, or later in my life, the restaurant franchise, pleasing the customer was paramount. Listening to the clients or guests, responding to them, and meeting their needs sustains the business. And mastering customer service, as well as sales, keeps the business pumped up every single day.

And early on, I noticed something about the fitness business. In January, buoyed by their New Year's resolutions, a spate of people would join. People were coming in two or three times a week to work out, lose weight, and lose flab to meet their New Year's resolutions. Wait time for the machines would increase, trainers were busy, and membership was spiking. Everything augured well for the coming year.

Like clockwork, in February and March, we'd see fast slippage. The members who signed up in January were already losing interest. They weren't motivated anymore to keep at their goals for losing weight, running, working out on the machines, or attending the classes. Enthusiasm would wane, and revenue projections, which looked so promising a month earlier, would plummet.

I didn't feel as if I were running a fitness center so much as a failed New Year's resolution. So there would be a rush of people in January, trying to start their year meeting their New Year's resolutions in January, and then membership would trail off. I needed a new strategy to lure people every month, not just when the calendar turned the page and a new year happened.

How could I stem the tide and keep members past the two months when their stamina evaporated and their interest waned? When I could invite them, give them a free month, and then let them get to know other members and form a fitness community, my membership would soar. I had to prove to prospective members that they'd make the most out of the club, that they'd have access to ample equipment and to trainers, no matter what month they joined.

By now our members had gotten to know me and knew I was the boss, and the more they knew me, the more they accepted me. That initial skepticism of "Are you the boss?" faded.

TIP #10
In Any Business, Getting to Know Your Customers Better Is a Crucial Aspect of Success

It isn't just pleasing the customers that contributes to the success of the business. Getting to know them better is just as important to retaining them the next day, the next month, the next year. And that was true for fitness centers, and later for doughnut shops, smoothie franchises, and pizza shops.

What I thought would work best was establishing a personal approach. Whenever I was at the club, I'd walk around and introduce myself to new members and also bring around the trainers and connect them with new members. The more the members linked up with trainers, established a routine, and formed relationships, the greater the chances they would stay and not escape when they forgot about their annual resolutions. Those relationships connected them to the club and often retained them.

Although I'm not a trained fitness instructor, while I was in the military I spent hours at the gym, so I was able to connect with clients through our shared passion for health and exercise. I'd walk around and introduce myself: "My name is Yonas Hagos, and I'm the owner." If I'd see them misusing a weight machine, I'd offer some tips.

Most times, they'd like getting to know the owner and listening to my suggestions. What I learned through experience was that many members liked getting to know me as the owner. It was a relatively small town where many people knew each other, and if they could say at lunch that "Yonas, the owner of Anytime, who's also a fitness instructor, trained me," it offered a certain cachet. Taking advantage of the fact that many members flocked to me, I became a ubiquitous presence and would stop to answer questions or help people with individual moves or exercises.

The more a relationship was cemented with members, the more intense their connection to the club became. That helped keep their good intentions or resolutions from melting away with the March thaw. It's equivalent to when the chef of a restaurant walks out of the kitchen, comes to the patron's table, and asks how the meal is. People love that personal touch from the boss, and they doesn't forget it easily. It makes the patrons feel special, or in my case the fitness members.

I was proving that concept in organizing regular workouts with members that I had gotten to know. I called them "my workout crew." It made us feel like a team. The ones who joined me on a regular basis, running, lifting weights, and doing aerobics, started seeing results. Once they saw themselves losing five pounds or racing (rather than struggling) up two flights of stairs, their enthusiasm spiked. The lesson here is that the owner's taking an individual role in the operations can boost business, create positive word of mouth, form relationships with guests, and have ramifications beyond the group. And that is true if the owner gets to know his or her customers at the dry-cleaning store, the secondhand clothing business, or the ice-cream shop.

Then I started to go beyond organizing physical workouts. I'd ask members individually, "What are your eating habits?" To those who told me they couldn't resist fried chicken and french fries, or cheeseburgers and nacho fries, I'd explain that if they were working out regularly and feeling fit, their eating habits didn't coincide with their fitness regimen. Diet and working out were inseparable, I told them—one feeds the other, at the risk of punning. The music and the lyrics didn't blend together. So the lesson here is the owner has to take an active role in operating the business at any level, and caring about the customers' health and well-being sends an indelible message. And that is true if it's a coffee shop, fitness center, or real estate office.

Every fitness member was different. Some dreamed of losing 50 pounds, though most just wanted to be healthy. Some seniors wanted to walk up the stairs without huffing and puffing. People wanted results, and if I could convince them to believe in delayed gratification, we'd have a much better chance of keeping them for a sustained period.

What I had to master to keep the Anytime Fitness Center pumping away (again, no pun intended) was selling techniques. I didn't earn an MBA or attend sales training, so I had to learn from experience and my own instincts.

TIP #11
Do the "Intel" to Figure Out Your Customers' Needs

One main thing I learned was if I kept my mouth shut and listened to my customers talk about what was on their minds, I could gather the necessary information, or "intel," to attract customers. So what was on my mind was seeing issues from their viewpoint. What motivated them to join the club? Was it all fitness? Finding friends? Finding a mate? Staying in shape? Acting on a resolution? Recommendation from a physician? Choosing my club because their friends were already members? The more I could ascertain why they chose Anytime, the more I could continue to meet their needs and retain them. About 60–66 percent of my clientele were female, and their needs were slightly different than those of the male members.

I also learned that figuring out customer needs and seeing issues from their vantage point was a lesson that could be carried over to restaurant franchises, or any other business, a kayak business, an app, a dating service—you name it.

For example, because our club operated 24/7, many female members, in particular, wanted to make sure it was safe to work out at late-night hours. To meet their needs, we offered them "panic" buttons to wear around their necks so they could contact 911 emergency immediately if something happened. That assuaged most members' fears. The members could pick one up from inside the club when they arrived and replace it when they left.

They also didn't want to be surrounded by grunting male weight lifters or guys who made judgments about their clothes or weight. We monitored our rooms to make sure that didn't happen. And they wanted their gym to be spotlessly clean. We assigned staff to make sure it was as spanking clean as possible.

One aspect of selling that I mastered is guerrilla marketing. Whenever there was an event or conference in our area, I made sure to attend to get the word out that our Anytime Fitness Center was a welcoming local establishment. If there was an event or conference within 25 miles, I'd show up with our brochures and introduce myself: "Hey, I'm Yonas, and I run and own the Anytime Fitness Center. We're here to meet your fitness needs." I wanted to humanize the center, letting people get to know me, know that there was someone there to turn to and connect with; that we were in this together. As with the cleaning-and-painting service, I'd get a slew of noes, but by this time, I paid them no mind.

Our monthly fee was $65, and members paid a one-time $35 fee for their key fob, which gained them entrance to the club after our normal business hours. The owners of the Anytime Fitness franchise encouraged us not to reduce or eliminate that key fob fee so that all the franchised units remained consistent. But, hey, I was running a business, and luring in new customers was one of my biggest goals.

At times, I'd offer members a deal of $20 for the key fob so they didn't have to pay $100 in their first check. The psychology behind this is nearly everyone loves a discount or deal. Whether extremely affluent, middle class, or working class, getting a discounted price can easily entice someone to want to join. Was I bending the franchise owner's rules? Well yes. But my commitment was making my franchise successful, and sometimes that took flexibility. I could, in fact, have waived the entire fee—but I was reluctant, because if word got out, it would antagonize other Anytime Fitness franchisees statewide.

When I joined the local chamber of commerce, started attending meetings, and began to get known in the community, it created much more name recognition for me and the fitness center. "That's Yonas, the guy who runs Anytime, and he's involved in the community" was the underlying sentiment. Once I started doing more for the community, giving to scholarships, getting involved in local high schools, it created a positive connection for the fitness center. Anytime Fitness's marketing plan underscored this point. Once I got past my resistance, the benefits mounted.

I also learned about the necessity of having sales skills. For any business, no matter the specialty, selling skills equal success. Most of us are selling ourselves all the time without ever realizing it. I was more of a soft salesperson than a hard seller, but I mastered playing up why my fitness center could meet members' needs and better their health and lives.

TIP #12
Highlight Your Competitive Edge

At the time, Anytime faced severe competition from several other national fitness centers, some of which charged its guests $9.99 a month with no initiation fee. So when prospective members asked me (and they did in droves) why they should join Anytime, which cost five or six times as much as competitors, I had ready answers—thanks to my newly acquired sales skills.

Our club had about 500 members, so during prime-time hours starting at 5 p.m. when most people stopped work, there would be 60 to 75 members working out. They had no problem getting stationary bicycles or treadmills, they didn't have to wait, and there was plenty of room in the exercise spaces. But some of those competitors, I told them, had thousands of members per club, so during prime time, there was a waiting list for the equipment. Most members want to jump into the exercise room and onto the bike or treadmill or lift weights. Who wants to wait for a stationary bicycle? That's worse than waiting on a Starbucks line.

Furthermore, some of our competitors would often limit treadmill use to half an hour. We had no limits. We offered more personal attention and unlimited time on the machines. And some of our competitors weren't open 24 hours a day.

My fitness trainers gave the first and sometimes second one-on-one fitness sessions for free to get to know and accommodate new members. Other fitness centers didn't have the resources to do so, and their fees were so small that they charged for everything.

"You get what you pay for," I told prospective members. "You get personal attention, flexibility, and accommodation."

On the flip side of our direct competition were the high-end centers. They catered to clients who invariably wore their fashionable workout gear, and they offered overpriced snack bars and trend-following classes. The culture at Anytime Fitness was more democratic and focused on the task at hand: exercise and wellness, and one didn't have to wear stylish workout attire or keep up with the Joneses to feel at home.

TIP #13
Help Your Clients Exceed Their Expectations

As an owner, I found that if I could enable my clients to exceed their expectations, it would make for a thriving fitness center. And that was a lesson that also carried over to my restaurant franchises. Making sure the coffee was always fresh, and never letting it sit around, was as important as assuring clients that their hard work on the stationary bicycle would pay off. You wouldn't lose 25 pounds a month, your cholesterol or blood pressure wouldn't dip overnight, but gradually, almost impercep- tibly, you'd reap results. It will happen, but it will require steady attendance over months, and that takes patience and fortitude.

TIP #14
Be the Brand

I was fit and thin and worked out regularly and watched what I ate. I wasn't only encouraging my clients what to do to achieve a healthy lifestyle; I was living it myself. "If Yonas, the owner, can do it, so can you" was my underlying message.

And part of embodying the brand was getting to know many of my members. I liked connecting with them; that was one of the secrets of the club's success. "Hey, John, how did your son's grad- uation go?" I'd ask. I strived to form bonds with as many guests as I could through training them, working out with them, chat- ting with them, and getting to know them. Just like on the old TV show *Cheers*, "where everybody knows your name," I encour- aged my trainers to greet each member by name and offer a wel- coming message.

TIP #15
Learn from the Competition

I also learned some things from my rivals. Once a week, one com- petitor would hold a Free Pizza night. I didn't do that once a week, but once a month, I'd organize a Free Pizza or Free Subway Sandwich, Free Drink, or Free Appetizer night so guests could meet one another and we'd connect more with them. The more customers got to know one another as friends or workout partners, the more the fitness club thrived. Also, people see free food as an unexpected benefit of joining the club.

TIP #16
Find Ways to Reduce Stress

In order to sustain my full-time job while running a fitness center part-time, something had to give. And that was basically my free time. Now that Kristie, my wife, was helping to run the club, I barely saw her. I continued to work the early shift at the plant. My workday was supposed to end at 3 p.m., but often I had to work overtime and was there until 5 and sometimes 7 p.m. Then I'd drive to the fitness center and help run it, or work with my crew as a trainer, or help with the bookkeeping, or clean, or do whatever else needed to be done.

Often, I didn't return home until midnight or later, and I had to be up at 3 a.m. some days, 4 a.m. other days, and 5 a.m. was late. I was working 18, 19, and sometimes 20 hours a day. You'd think I'd have collapsed, but I had the verve and passion to make this franchise work. I knew I couldn't sustain this pace forever, and my wife was saying, "You're going to burn out, get run down, or overdo it." And my wife is almost always right.

I didn't sleep much. But that's where my military training came in handy. When I was in the Army and overseas, we never slept much; yet we had to be limber, focused, and ready for action. Somehow that became a habit and part of my system. But if you didn't spend time in the armed services, my advice would be to lead a straight and narrow life in order to sustain your energy. Go to sleep early, don't overdo liquor, and work out (whether you own a fitness center or not); maintain balance in your life. You're going to have to muster all the energy within you to get your new venture up and running.

Learning to delegate helped reduce some stress. We hired someone part-time to do the cleaning, and that helped. Then we engaged in some old fashioned bartering, a term that seemingly has gone out of style, where we offered free memberships for people in exchange for their performing some other tasks.

TIP #17
Reward Your Top Performers

As an example: Nicole, our sales manager, was integral to expanding my business. She was skilled and engaging, and she was enrolling 30 members a month, sometimes 40 and at times 50. That meant the money started rolling in. And since she earned a good salary and gained commissions on each new member, she was making a healthy salary and deserved every dollar of it.

Key to running a successful franchise is promoting your talented employees and establishing a career path. That said volumes of what made our Dunkin' Donuts franchise successful, and what ultimately sustained them through ups and downs and through recessions and upheavals and pandemics. One of the first things I said to prospective employees was, "Where do you see yourself going in two years? Five years? What's your long-term plan? Are you committed to the restaurant industry?" If they weren't committed, that could be fine, too, since young people change paths and many college students aren't definitive about where they want to be in the future. But for those who were, and those who had the right temperament and skills to be a cashier or sales associate, my major pitch was, "If you prove competent, we'll help you to grow and move up." Creating that career path, sticking to it, training people, and showing them what it took to advance to the next level was one of the differentiating factors that made our Dunkin' Donuts locations thrive.

Sales associates, for example, were promoted to shift leads, at more money and responsibility. And then they'd step up and become shift managers, then move to assistant managers, general managers, and multiunit managers, and then advance to area directors. For staff who were bright, eager, ambitious, and competent, there was endless opportunity to blossom and prosper.

TIP #18
Make Sure Managers Are Treating Their Staff Well

Ultimately, a business is only as good as the managers who oversee their staff.

When I was overseeing matters at the Normal, Illinois, Dunkin', I noticed that the manager spent a lot of time conversing with employees about their social lives, as if she were their friend, not their boss. She also played favorites. Some of them got on her good side, could do little wrong, and rarely received any constructive feedback but just coasted; and some got on her bad side, could do little right, rarely received any positive reinforcement, and were chastised for almost everything. Though she was knowledgeable, she didn't treat the staff equitably, and that led to low morale, particularly with the unfavored staff.

To see if I could salvage the situation, I thought a change of scenery could cure her drawbacks and weaknesses. I named her manager of the new store, and I began to take charge of the other store myself to see if I could revive morale. But soon after the new store opened, she got into some disputes with some of the employees and faced some emotional upheavals with employees, and so the change of scenery, alas, didn't alter her way of managing the staff. She came across as seeking out drama, and that personality won't work in running a restaurant franchise, which needs a steady captain at the helm. Eventually, she was fired.

As I noted above, I decided to take over the reins in the store in Normal. My goal in standing in as manager was to restore the trust of the staff, which had been damaged. I went out of my way to ensure that every staff member was treated the same, set rules and regulations that everyone was to follow, recognized all the staff for engaging in customer-friendly behaviors, and led from the front. Once the staff saw that everyone was now on equal standing, trust started to grow and morale rose. I established an open-door policy where anyone on staff, no matter their job title or ranking, could come to me with an issue, and it would be discussed and resolved.

TIP #19
Inspire Customer Loyalty

One key thing I learned running the fitness center for nearly three years was that everyone has a unique personality. I had to "read" the person—get a sense of the person—and discover what worked and what didn't. The more I knew about what motivated a person, the more I could understand and unlock the person's character and find a solution to a problem or conflict.

I also learned a considerable amount about the art of self-promotion and how it is not a bad thing to highlight your accomplishments, especially if you can show they make you a better owner of your business. If a member liked me or admired me personally, most often that member would sign the contract for a year. If members felt my values and experiences aligned with theirs, trust followed, and that meant customer loyalty. I had to master earning their trust, which, at first, didn't come naturally. The more I could individualize my pitch, the better. I pushed some of my humility to the side and told people my story about coming to the States, spending time in the Army, and, of course, being awarded my Purple Heart.

Sure, every New Year's at Anytime Fitness, we'd see a throng of new members trying to live up to their resolutions. But signing up new members is one thing; retaining them for the second and third year is something else. What I learned early is that the fitness center has to be fully engaged with each member to keep the person on board.

Every March, one member or another would track me down, ask if I was the owner, and then tell me she joined three months earlier, hadn't come in for two months, and wanted to cancel her membership because she didn't see results. I'd tell her first that she signed a contract for a year, ask her to give it a chance, and arrange a free fitness session with one of my trainers. I found if I could set up a structure to keep members involved for the first three months, get them into the gym regimen until they saw some temporary results, I could hook them for the long haul. But it takes time, repeated exercise, and changing one's diet, and that can take months.

At Anytime Fitness, we'd often offer guests a free training session to get them involved and engaged. Sometimes they would pay for an additional two or three sessions to really get into a rhythm. Then I'd encourage my staff to make follow-up calls. "How's it going? What's working? What's not?" The point was to show we cared and were involved in their everyday activities.

Too many members made excuses about why they weren't attending the gym regularly. "I'm too busy, working out isn't my top priority, and I have other things to do." Sure, we all have many priorities. But if I could get them to come in three times a week, get into the rhythm, and get fit, the odds of retaining them soared.

LOOKING FORWARD AND LOOKING BACK

Finally In 2010, the gym, after a year or so, started to turn a profit. But I knew I couldn't sustain working at a full-time job and running a fitness center. I needed a better solution if this club were going to survive under my ownership.

In 2011, I decided to sell the club. I wanted to pursue my real dream of getting involved in restaurant franchising. Food is a necessity, especially affordable delicious food. What I learned from having to close my painting-and-cleaning business is that gym memberships are not a necessity, but a luxury. I wanted to own a business that could be more sustainable in a recession or other unforeseen downturn. This decision led me to my next endeavor.

When people ask me if they should leave their structured job, which pays, for example, $100,000 a year, and plunge into starting their own business, I usually tell them about owning my first fitness franchise and how I didn't give up my secure job for the franchise itself. It was a "both/and" situation and time in my life. I'd often start working at the plant at 5 a.m. and often work a 12-hour shift, and then I'd head to the gym and work until 9 p.m. or later. Can you spell "very long days"? And that included weekends for the first year. There were no days off, no vacations, and only an occasional holiday—and even those were rare because the fitness business stayed open nearly every day but Christmas.

This was my life for more than a year, and I didn't complain. If I wanted weekends off, I would have strived to attain some nine-to-five job, but that wasn't my path. I'd tell potential entrepreneurs that they were relinquishing their security, their weekends off, their regular paychecks, to plunge into the abyss of not knowing how everything would turn out.

By nature, I'm an introvert. But owning a fitness center turned me into more of an extrovert. I always say to people now,

"If you don't like talking to people, consider a warehouse job, where you can keep your distance from most folks."

Owning and working at a fitness center entails becoming involved with people on a day-to-day basis. "How are you doing, Jack, on the weights? Are you looking forward to your daughter's high school graduation?" Getting to know people, not just their exercise regimens but also their personal lives, went a long way toward keeping them involved and making Anytime Fitness a community. If you're in the people business—and that can encompass fitness centers, doughnut shops, and burger joints—you have to reach out. The more effervescent and upbeat I was, the more it sent a message to my guests and employees that we were all in this together.

I was thin, I worked out, and I watched my diet, and many guests would say, "What do I have to do to look like you?"

"It's a mindset," I would tell them. "Work out regularly. Like what you do. Eat well. Cut down on sweets. I guarantee you'll feel better about yourself. The mind and body are interconnected."

In many ways, I became the brand. I worked out, stayed fit, ate in a (mostly) healthy way, and tried to embody what Anytime Fitness represented: being fit, having fun and staying healthy. It all fit together.

CHAPTER 5

THE WAY TO EXPAND

*Make the First Restaurant or Business
Succeed and Move on from There*

W hen I was running Anytime Fitness Center, I learned a major truth. Most people crave instant gratification. At the fitness center, members could spend weeks lifting weights, doing squats, and running 20 minutes on a treadmill and wouldn't necessarily lose any weight, or they felt the loss was negligible. Making a difference could take weeks, if not more, and also required changing one's diet, cutting out sugar and carbohydrates, reducing pizza intake, and forgoing puddings and cake. And that was considered a sacrifice.

I started thinking about immediate gratification. At a fast-food chain like Dunkin' Donuts (whose name was streamlined to

Dunkin' in 2020), all a customer had to do was spend under $5 in exchange for a doughnut and coffee to receive instant satisfaction. It didn't take hours on the fitness floor or lots of time on the treadmill, and the customer was happy. How appealing was that idea for a would-be entrepreneur?

And retaining customers at Dunkin' was more predictable. As long as the chain could provide fresh food and tasty coffee and serve the guests as quickly as possible, the odds are they would be happy and would return. And that didn't require a month of workouts, psychological coaching, and a dietary cutback. You bite into a doughnut, appreciate the sugary taste, get a rush, and pronto, you're happy for about $5 or less!

In part for some of these very reasons, it takes a considerable amount of capital to acquire a restaurant franchise like Dunkin' Donuts. It also takes know-how and experience. And that's the one thing that I had: years of part-time jobs working in fast-food eateries, followed by my managerial and ownership experience of the fitness center. What I learned about taking care of the customer when I was 14 years old paid off 13 years later, when I was close to owning my first franchise.

As I explained in earlier chapters, growing up in Illinois, I worked in a series of entry-level jobs in several fast-food franchises. At age 14, I started at McDonald's, and at age 15 moved to Burger King, where I worked on and off for four years. So owning a restaurant franchise tapped my prior experience, harkened back to my youth, and resonated with me since I had been trained and groomed by a variety of managers. "Go with what you know," I said to myself.

And then in 2008, I saw an ad for a Domino's Pizza franchising program that started participants off in a five-week training program. Based on my background as a shift manager at Burger King, I secured a spot in the program at a Domino's in Naperville,

Illinois—operated by a powerhouse of a franchisee named Ray Montez. He became one of my first franchising role models since he owned 17 Domino's Pizzas in the Chicago suburbs. And like me, he was a hardworking, gritty kind of guy.

During the five-week training program, I learned the ins and outs of operating a Domino's Pizza franchise, including how to make a pizza, how to open and close a location, how to organize running a shift, how to take an order, and how to make sure everything is moving smoothly. Hence, I learned a number of invaluable skills to make a business work, whether it was a restaurant franchise, a moving van service, an app, or a food truck. Take your time and get the job done right. For Domino's the lesson was making sure the ingredients in the pizza all cohered. Rushing it can come back to haunt you and ruin the customer experience. Get the job done right, and impart that to your staff.

I also got to ask an assortment of questions to Montez. When I asked him how he managed to own 17 Domino's Pizzas, his response made me laugh. "I worked my butt off; that's how. Are you willing to sleep in the store?" he asked me, and I could see how blood, sweat, and tears were critical to his success. I vowed to follow in his footsteps.

I was close to getting married to Kristie, and that likely prompted my supervisor to ask, "So, Yonas, what's your next move? I know you don't see yourself working at the plant for the next 30 years?"

Since he was a friend and not just a colleague, I was straight with him. "I'm going to look into opening a restaurant franchise," I replied. "For a guy like me, that's the quickest way to make a steady income and become my own boss."

"If you do, count me in, and my buddy. We're both looking to invest. We'll help you open it up, and you can run it while we keep our steady jobs," he said. It was as if a lightning bolt had struck, since combining with them made it easier to finance the venture, and I likely couldn't have raised enough funds without them. And yet I could be running the show, and they were the hidden investors. How lucky was I?

Finding the right investors is doable for just about everyone. We all know someone who has money who likely knows our strengths and weaknesses. Insiders call this technique of tapping your friends and family for capital investment as "finding the right angels," and that's what it often takes to build up enough money to acquire your first franchise. In most cases, you're not only paying the $40,000 or $50,000 royalty fee to the franchise, the franchise initial fees, but there are capital improvement costs, construction costs, equipment fees, and more, adding up to $325,000 in our case, and it could be more for loftier franchises.

It's the angels who are friends and family who are apt to lend money and invest in your business. Of course, that expenditure requires a well-developed business plan and a strategy to earn back their money. No one wants to lose the funding of one's friends and family, so maximizing success is critical.

Another way of obtaining funding is through a local bank, but that is a much trickier proposition. Banks prefer giving loans to people with solid track records of success, not neophytes. Banks scrutinize their financing very intensively and often ask for collateral to lessen their risk. And that holds as true for franchisees as it does for fitness center entrepreneurs.

Many people who are starting out ask me if restaurant experience is required to achieve success in a chain franchise. Having a track record of success as a manager, no matter what the industry, helps heighten the chances of doing well. For example, managing a fitness center enabled me to shift into restaurant management.

Many restaurants have "Help Wanted" signs in their window for entry-level jobs, and if you are interested in franchise success, my advice would be to get hired and work there for at least six months to a year. I'd also urge you to try out as many jobs as possible: host, waiter, cashier, supervisor, back of the house—they all contribute to learning the inner workings of a restaurant. Ask about cross-training and learning as many jobs as possible. Learn the espresso station, the egg station, the drive-through; try as many roles as possible. If you like what you see, consider launching and investing in a franchise.

But restaurant ownership isn't for everyone because it is so demanding and unrelenting, often seven days a week, often mornings, afternoons, and nights, and weekends and holidays—the beat keeps moving on and on. Running a restaurant becomes a lot easier if you see how the facility works from all viewpoints.

At the core of everything for me was one driving idea: I wanted to be my own boss. I liked my job at the utility plant and had few complaints. But deep down inside, I wanted to be self-employed. I wanted to work for myself. I figured if I worked harder than anyone else, I could reap the rewards, rather than being a salaried worker and earning a limited amount. Becoming an entrepreneur felt like being free, being able to call my own shots, making the rules rather than having to follow them.

At the time, many of my friends were incredulous that I was starting the Dunkin' franchisee process. "You can't do that," one friend said to me.

"You'll never be able to raise that much money," another (so-called) friend exclaimed.

Of course, the more they doubted me, the harder I worked to make it happen. "I'm going to show you that I'm going to make it," I thought to myself. Their resistance and skepticism fueled my desire to succeed. Nothing was going to stop me now.

And for an immigrant like me, who didn't have a graduate degree, or for that matter, a bachelor's degree, restaurant franchise ownership was a natural path to success. As I've written, I started my career in fast-food eateries as a 14-year-old, a path that many immigrants take. We start with entry level roles such as fast-food cashier, dishwasher, janitor. We start at the bottom, prove that we can work hard, and try to move up a notch or two, to become a line chef, or building manager, or supervisor. So for me, the road went from flipping burgers to overseeing the franchise.

Why did Dunkin' Donuts interest and resonate for me? It was personal. When I was 10 years old or so, my dad and I would stop there on a Sunday morning. He worked hard and long, so we weren't able to spend much time together during the week. Weekends at Dunkin' was our time.

We'd talk about politics, what was going on locally; and he'd describe to me what it was like driving a cab in Chicago, the people he met in the taxi, the places he stopped, the Greek diners where he grabbed his dinner before returning to the taxi. So Dunkin' Donuts always meant childhood memories of bonding with my dad. That emotional memory struck deep into my core. Nonetheless, my interesting in becoming its franchisee was a business decision, not something nostalgic based on my past.

When I started exploring which restaurant franchise to invest in, other factors leaped into view. McDonald's prevailed as the gold standard for fast-food dining and buying into a franchise. Once you became a franchisee there, you could mess it up and ruin it, but in most cases, you were on the pathway to success. And running one McDonald's expertly usually resulted in opening a second and maybe a third, and then you were on to the beeline to major satisfaction and steady income. But the reality of becoming a McDonald's franchisee was that you wait at the end of a long line to be considered. It could likely be a yearlong wait before your application was to be considered, and waiting that long made me feel uncomfortable, so I moved on.

Then I explored franchising a Buffalo Wild Wings outlet. How many people aged 21–34 could resist the allure of chicken wings, chicken tenders, chicken sandwiches, and beer, all while watching your favorite team play college football on Saturdays, NFL football on Sundays, or baseball, or basketball, or hockey? Few could, so I looked into launching one of those eateries, but they too had a long waiting list, and I was eager to get out of the starting gate.

And then I got the call that changed my life. One of my partners called me one morning, an unexpected twinkle in his voice. "Hey, Yonas, you gotta hear this. Do you know where I am? Of course you don't. I'm at a Dunkin' Donuts waiting in line. The line of cars for the drive-through is around the block. There must be 15 cars lined up. This could take 15 minutes or maybe 20 minutes to get my order. Is that the best news you ever heard?" he exclaimed laughing. "Forget waiting in line for McDonald's or Buffalo Wild Wings. Get thee to a Dunkin' franchise office," he suggested.

Then I started to do my own research on Dunkin'. My exploration said that about 70 percent of its revenue was generated between 5 a.m. and 11 a.m., and then business trailed off. I got the contact information for opening a Dunkin' Donuts franchise, and then the emailing started, and this took two months or so, at the least, to get started in filling out forms, and six months before I submitted all the necessary paperwork.

Opening a business requires doing the research, and even the legwork, to do the due diligence to know more about the venture you're exploring. Know as much about the ins and outs of its business as you can. The more knowledgeable you are, the better your questions will be, and businesses, particularly franchises, want to work with people who do their homework and are prepared for their new venture.

And I also had some luck that played a role. Yes, I had some personal connection to Dunkin' based on my background, but this was a business decision. When my brother was attending college, he worked part time to earn money for a Dunkin' Donuts franchisee who owned several units and was interested in selling one of them. So the timing was perfect. As we were moving through the franchisee acceptance line, and our SBA and JPMorgan Chase loan was gaining acceptance, the owner was looking to sell. My brother ultimately got $25,000 as a referral fee, so he came up a winner, too.

I also established a very positive rapport with Curtis Roberts, who was the director of Dunkin' Donuts' Midwest franchises. He was very straight with me, very firm, accepted no guff, and acted like the drill sergeant I encountered in the Army, firm and forceful and direct. That worked for me based on my military background.

My partners and I needed to raise $325,000 to open the Dunkin' franchise. To raise the money, the three of us secured an SBA loan for about $100,000, raised about $100,000 from an outside investor, and then my two partners and I together invested about $125,000 of our own money. For us, that was a healthy sum, but not an impossible one. So both of the franchises I had invested in, at this point, the fitness center and Dunkin', cost about $300,000 to get them off the ground.

I met with my accountant to tell him that I'd be cashing in some of my 401(k) plan to generate enough cash to provide my share of the money needed to meet our franchisee agreement. He reviewed the financial documents, and while admittedly, he was on the cautious side, he advised me that most Dunkin' franchises prospered and I was on the right track. His support and knowledge of finances and taxes went a long way in supporting my initial investment.

I also paid a price for withdrawing funds early from my 401(k) plan. I was hit with a tax penalty of about 30 percent, which hurt in the pocketbook. It was a hefty price to pay, but I needed to draw on those funds to open that franchise, so I had to bite the bullet and pay the price.

Finally, with the help of my two partners and my own investment, we capitalized the full amount. Now we had to get through the Dunkin' vetting process, which entailed a series of interviews with several of the company's department heads over a sustained period. This was an exhaustive, painstaking, rather elaborate process to determine if we were the right partners to fit the franchisee.

And yet Curtis Roberts kept saying, "Don't worry. With the SBA loan and injecting your own money, you'll be fine." He kept saying the criterion was about more than money. "It's about someone who can operate the franchise and make it a success. And you have the right background. You've owned a franchise and made it successful, and you started working in fast-food establishments as a teenager, so you know the drill," he explained.

"We want our operators to be in it for the long term," Roberts disclosed to us. In fact, many franchisee agreements, such as the ones with Dunkin' Donuts, encompassed 20 years (some franchise contracts lasted 10 years). Of course, if the franchisee wasn't performing well, most chains would buy the franchisee out and terminate the lease early, which is to everyone's benefit.

Roberts also suggested that the three of us do our homework. Read about the history of the company, see how it started, what led to its development. "Do your research on knowing the ins and outs of the brand's history," he urged us. He wanted us to do well, and he served as one of our mentors. Yes, our goal was to understand the process, what the company's core identity was, and then strive to be in sync with what it was trying to achieve.

Then we also had to develop our own Dunkin' Donuts business plan, of how we'd be operating, whom we'd be targeting, and how we'd treat our employees.

Of course, we faced some financial risk. I figured the worst thing that could happen if we failed was that Dunkin' Donuts would take the store over, and we'd lose money but would keep our mortgage, and I'd keep the rest of my savings. Life's a risk, and I was just trying to minimize any losses and reap some gains.

The partnership with my two colleagues was like a marriage. Decisions were made jointly, we talked things over, and we shared the oversight, but I ran the franchise day-to-day. Until the day I die, I will always be thankful to these two buddies. One of them is still involved in several of my businesses as a financial partner, and the other one stepped away and absolved himself of ownership. But they believed in a 28-year-old immigrant, who was just starting out as an entrepreneur. They saw a spark in me that was ready to ignite and provided much of the financial capital to get me into franchise ownership. I will always be indebted to them.

When I applied, the franchising manager responded promptly and arranged a telephone interview with me. "The vetting process has begun," I thought to myself. I had filled him in on my extensive background in the fast-food industry. I started as a cook at McDonald's, became a cashier, and then went on to become a shift leader at Burger King, and I described my managerial experience running Anytime Fitness. He seemed to be impressed, and the next step, he said, was checking my financial background. It would take numerous interviews with several department heads over a lengthy period for this process to reach its conclusion.

That was the first interview of what would become five discussions with Dunkin's senior franchising managers with me and my two partners. Applying to an Ivy League college couldn't have been this intense. We eventually met with executives in operations, development, marketing, and construction who all wanted to learn about our plans, our intentions, and our backgrounds. They wanted to know how we intended to run a Dunkin' outlet, and they asked specific questions about the business plan we developed.

Often, these interviews are conducted by a team from operations, construction, and development who barrage you with questions to get a stronger sense of whether you're a good fit with Dunkin' or another franchise. In our case, though, we were only queried by the heads of the departments. It was manageable, and we were prepared.

The Dunkin' Donuts vetting process was intensive, involved, and prolonged, taking place over a one-year period. In many ways, it's like a marriage, because the franchisee is joining forces with the parent company. Hence, the people at Dunkin' wanted to make sure we could all get along, and we had the right temperament to become a Dunkin' franchisee and be in this endeavor for the long haul. What they were trying to avoid was choosing franchisees who couldn't make it, couldn't sustain the revenue goals, couldn't established rapport with customers, and left the business quickly. Could we listen? Solve problems? Deal with unruly customers? Handle staff and get the most out of them? These were the underlying questions that drove their interrogations.

Then they wanted to know who of the team was going to operate the business, which was me. So they queried me on my background, my restaurant experience. They wanted to know who my mentors were and whom I learned from. I was 30 years old at the time in 2013. But still I was able to discuss my extensive franchise restaurant experience from Burger King, talking about the three managers who shaped my vision of what it takes to run a successful eatery. I talked about what I learned about handling disgruntled customers, how I learned to problem-solve, making working in a restaurant fun even though it was hard, and what it took to create a winning culture for employees and customers.

So having the money in place was only a starting point. We had to prove to them that we had the smarts to operate the business and make it a success.

For example, they asked me questions about how I ran the Anytime Fitness branch, focusing on how I handled conflicts with customers and employees and how the staff and I got along with the community. Their goal was to make sure we had the right temperament to run a franchise, get along with the community and customers, and represent the brand in a positive way. Based on my extensive background in both restaurants and the fitness franchise, I felt I answered the questions effectively. It's important that when you enter these discussions, you maintain your composure, demonstrate a calm presence, and show that you can handle questions without ever losing your temper or getting bent out of shape.

All these questions probing my temperament revealed key issues of what it takes to operate a Dunkin's location successfully. All the interviewers were trying to do was to determine if we were a good fit, could handle the operations, treat customers right, and solve problems.

I also learned several underlying truths during the franchisee interviews including the following:

1. **Don't oversell your experience if it's not aligned with the demands of the business.** Be realistic about what you can accomplish. Make sure you can raise the necessary amount of capital and have the requisite managerial background, either in the restaurant business or elsewhere.

2. **Get your boots on the ground.** Understand the inside scoop on what it takes to run a restaurant franchise in terms of the hours required on-site, the persistent interaction with customers and employees, and all the processes such as ordering food and preparing it that are demanded in the restaurant business.

I knew that the stakes were high in running that first Dunkin'. Mark Levine was the director of development at Dunkin', and he counseled and mentored me (he recently retired). But he also said to me, "Yonas, that first franchise you open is pivotal. If it's a home run, you can move on and open a second one. But if it's a dud, it could end your franchise career before it gets off the ground." I had been warned.

And the site we were looking into was a little complicated. It was situated near a shopping center, which, of course, is good because that meant plenty of traffic and customers who needed caffeine, a doughnut, and/or an egg sandwich to start their day. It was also off Interstate 55, a busy thoroughfare in the Normal area. But the site had four houses on it, though zoned for commercial use, and we needed to acquire one of them, demolish it, and then build a new Dunkin' franchise. We ended up buying one house with a lowball figure of $350,000, because we were coming out of a recession and real estate prices had plunged. Luckily for us, the timing helped make the site affordable. It was a one-acre lot, exactly what we needed.

Savvy Levine pointed out, in his real estate lingo, "You want to be in their way and on their way," which meant people would pass the Dunkin' on the way into the shopping mall and getting onto Interstate 55, so it was a win-win. But it's a lesson to be learned for any business. Being in a pedestrian-heavy site downtown, or in a shopping center strip, or near a university can boost business.

"If you could run a gym for two years, you can sell doughnuts and coffee," Roberts assured me. Still, the interview process
was rigorous. In fact, as I noted above, my partners and I had five
interviews. And in those interviews, I told the Dunkin' folks about
creating a culture, making it fun, developing rapport with everyone, and making the work more like teamwork than drudgery.

My partners had bigger bank accounts than I did so they
injected more capital, but because of both my franchise experience and my dream to run a franchise, I was going to be the one
running the show, even if I had financial backers. Finally we were
able to sign for the Dunkin' Donuts franchise in Normal.

Now my two partners and I were ready for training. All three
of us opted to participate so we'd get to know what makes a
franchise click and prosper. Then for five weeks, my partners
and I participated in Dunkin' Donuts' five-week training, learning what works, how to handle customers, and what the protocols are for running a franchise. The company even sent us to
Orlando to train at a Dunkin' model franchise.

We participated in just about every job you could name:
cashier, crew member, and manager. We learned how to prep the
food and were offered pointers when we were on the floor about
the best techniques to manage employees. It was like in the military where you learn every job just in case you have to step in
and perform it. The company wanted us to be prepared for any
encounter to know how to handle it, and the underlying motto
was "no surprises."

We also interacted with customers, and the Dunkin' supervisors would point out how to develop a rapport with each guest.
We even learned how to count the money at the end of the day, a
critical component in running a successful operation.

The unstated message was that the owner/operator has to
see the restaurant from every possible vantage point. This meant

making sure the owner was cross-trained. Knowing how to make the doughnuts, open the restaurant, close the store, prepare it for the next day, and close at night was all covered. Since restaurants traditionally face a slew of turnover, knowing every job and what it entails is critical to filling in when someone leaves.

We also learned high-level strategies that transcended the day-to-day operations, such as how to read financial statements, how to budget, how to forecast using information that Dunkin' provided, and how to project revenue for one day based on last year's data to project when and how many employees are needed. I can see what revenue I generated on April 14 and determine how to adjust my staff on that day the next year.

It's a crash course, no doubt about that. In five weeks, you can only learn so much, but you master the basics. It teaches you what to look for, what to concentrate on, and what pitfalls to avoid.

One of the major skills that we were taught in the training was the secret steps to making good coffee. When you own a Dunkin' Donuts franchise, strong, tasty, fresh, well-made java is key to running a thriving outlet. When I think of Dunkin', good coffee and those sugary doughnuts come to my mind first.

We were trained to use filtered water only, because the fresher the water, the better the coffee. We were taught to measure the amount of coffee we used to ensure that it was the precise right amount. And then we were trained to make new coffee every three or four hours and no later than that to ensure freshness. We also had to calibrate the equipment and make sure the grinder was cleaned out, the coffeemaker was clean, and fresh coffee was kept in the pot for no more than an hour.

In fact, it would take 2 minutes and 32 seconds (and needless to say, that is exact!) to brew to its ultimate taste.

One other secret about running a Dunkin' franchise. In the eighties, a character actor named Lou Jacobi starred in the chain's advertisement as a beleaguered franchise owner who would arise in the wee hours of the morning and grumble, "Time to make the doughnuts." It became such a catchphrase that 40 years later, customers, and even some employees, will still wake up early and mutter, "Time to make the doughnuts." But the truth is, in order to make the chain more efficient, dough-nuts were made daily at a central commissary and delivered each morning to the specific franchise. They arrived at the franchise prebaked, and then were finished off in the oven for a few min-utes to ensure freshness.

No doubt this was a crammed course for a week, jamming in all the details it requires to operate a Dunkin' that could easily have been stretched out into 10 weeks.

What most trainees didn't realize during their one-week experience was that the Dunkin' franchise manager was observ-ing and evaluating every trainee. For many Dunkin' franchisers, owning multiple locations was the goal, so the franchise manager was observing which franchisees took the training easily, incor-porating all the techniques, and which resisted them.

Once I completed the training, I was told that some franchi-sees came across as too cocky, as if they knew everything and the training was beneath them. This damaged their reputation. On the other hand, others operated as students who wanted to learn as much as possible and master all the intricate details of mak-ing a good cup of coffee or an egg sandwich, which impressed the Dunkin' executives. For the trainees who were cavalier and felt as if they knew more than the Dunkin' leaders, this was their kiss of death and would lead to them being cut off from owning more than one location The point is, character matters. No mat-ter what the business is.

Dunkin' management also paired us with a nearby existing franchisee, and here we hit the jackpot. We were referred to Sim

Patel, who owned several Dunkin' locations in the Illinois sub-urbs, not far from ours. He invited me to one of his locations, gave me his personal email address and his cell phone number, and urged me to text if a problem arose. Some people say, "Call me if you need me," but don't mean it, but he did.

In many other businesses, you won't be able to meet with an owner of a similar enterprise. So what you can do instead is go to YouTube and Google and do your homework there to learn what it takes to, say, run a small mailbox shop or oil and lube place. Nowadays you can find anything on the internet, often includ-ing videos.

Patel, who was also an immigrant, identified with me. I was a 28-year-old immigrant who must have reminded him of him-self starting out. I was eager, enthusiastic, filled with promise and wonder, and wanted to soak up as much information as possible. Succeeding was in my veins just as my blood streamed through me, and I'm sure Patel sensed it.

"I'm here to help you," he said. "Whatever you need, I'm here for you."

I learned a lot of specific tools from Patel. For example, the first Dunkin' that he acquired had been generating $8,000 weekly, which didn't pay all the bills, and he turned it around to the point where it was racking up $60,000 a week. When I asked him what triggered the turnaround, one main factor he pointed to was investing in the franchise. The previous owner had stopped injecting new capital and buying new equipment and was coasting, and it turns out, he was running it into the ground. Hence, it's always wise to put money into a business when you're doing well. That's the time to boost revenue.

Everything Patel did was about upgrading the customer experience at Dunkin' Donuts. He emphasized hiring the right staff, and then training them sufficiently and giving them some time to ease into their job, and he underscored delivering a quality product to every customer.

Patel introduced a new system, whose aim was to speed things up, since drive-throughs were playing an increasingly potent role in each Dunkin's success. He made sure that the expiration dates on all the products were adhered to, and anything stale or not fresh was discarded. "Everything has a shelf life," he told me. The fresher the product, the more it appealed to Dunkin's customers. When it came to food preparation, he trained his staff to take the eggs out of the refrigerator, put them into a clean container, and, for health reasons, place them into the cooler. They can't sit outside because they'd spoil too easily. But that way, they'd be ready for cooking the next day.

The other thing about Patel that stood out was that no matter what happened and how difficult matters became, he stayed positive. He never had that "Woe is me" attitude that you hear from many franchisees who seem overwhelmed and can't keep up with the pressure of balancing five balls in the air at once. No matter what happened, including the dreaded pandemic, Patel felt as if he was one step ahead and showed gratitude. The message was, "How lucky am I to be living in America, where people are safe and where order prevails, instead of back home, where chaos rules." He never let go of that positive feeling, and I've tried hard to adopt that same attitude. Of course, he too may have had his bad days or setbacks, but I never spotted them.

Patel also gave me the inside scoop on how he treated his employees. "Treat people the way you want to be treated," he urged me. I've adopted that as one of my mantras.

Another factor in running a successful franchise I learned early on was the necessity to take care of the equipment. It's easy to let the espresso machine get rusty and not pay attention to the blender's malfunctioning. I also learned to invest in machinery, which can be pricey. Buying a second espresso machine for $12,000 is costly, but that enables staff to make two cups at a time rather than having the customer wait for each one to be completed.

I learned early on that Americans are in a rush; no one wants to wait. If the drive-through line was backed up with 10 cars, the customer would move on to Starbucks to see if its queue was shorter. Waiting in life for four minutes feels like an eternity to some customers, which we understood. Faster, quicker, more efficient wins the coffee and breakfast battles in the morning, and I wanted Dunkin' Donuts to prevail over its many competitors. The faster I could serve my customers, the more guests flocked to us, and the higher were the profits. Orders had to be executed perfectly. And that's the bottom line.

To make sure the order was handled correctly, we installed a system where each staffer would verify the request to the customer. "Large coffee with milk and one sugar and one glazed doughnut," the attendant would repeat to ensure accuracy. And, in fact, to hasten the pace, Dunkin' has been exploring building two drive-through windows.

How did this need for speed affect loyalty? Sure, even without the focus on speed, likely we would still have retained our loyal customers who came through the drive-through every day. But I always felt we were on the spot and had to deliver that quick service each day. And it isn't just at fast-food eateries. Most businesses need to deliver their services as quickly and expertly as possible, or the consumer will walk. We're in an age of instant gratification, fueled by immediate responses from our smartphones, and it's hard to get around that.

During the Dunkin' training, the message that was conveyed was treat the customer as the boss. Without the customers, we can't keep the doors open. Pleasing the customers, getting their orders right, being polite, getting to know them, delivering an excellent product became the guiding principles for every guest interaction. If we could get the customer through the drive through in five minutes or less, we'd snare that customer and bring him or her back the next day.

Just as I learned at the fitness center, I'd train my staff to develop as many customer relationships as possible. You didn't have to be best friends with people or elicit any intimate details of their lives, but getting to know their names sent a strong message. "Hey, Dan, how are you doing today? How did your son's football game go?" Establishing that rapport with the customers, where they knew me or my employees, went a long way to retaining them. And accomplishing this conversation while getting them through the drive-through line in breakneck speed took some ingenuity.

And I liked getting to know my clientele. It made the customers feel as if they belonged and they were special to us. Which, of course, they were. And it made me feel part of a community. So, yes, it was good for business, but it also felt encouraging and rewarding to know my customers. At a time post-pandemic, when so many people were isolated and disconnected, this connecting with customers assumed an even more important role. For some customers who were isolated, that human contact made their day. And for all customers, knowing an employee's name, a manager's name, an owner's name, drew them back repeatedly.

If I observed my staffers, such as Ronette and Muriel, getting to know a customer, I might order a pizza and treat those staffers to lunch as validation for carrying out our customer goals. "You did a good job today. I like the way you've been addressing our clientele. It sends a strong message," I'd say to them, trying to reinforce their behavior. And they'd tell their colleagues, and the momentum would start to build. We wanted the customer to think, "This Dunkin' treats its customers the right way."

Conversely, if a staffer made a mistake with an order, I'd take him or her aside and try to perform a course correction. "Hey, Ronnie, we need to get the egg sandwich order right every time. Tomorrow, pay more attention. We need to keep those errors to a minimum." I wanted to make sure the problem was addressed but didn't want to bash or humiliate the employee. There's no reason to hurt or belittle your employees. Just focus on correcting the miscue, move on to the next order, and be done with it.

My goal here wasn't to chastise the employee but to make sure we were building relationships with customers and getting their orders right. That was key. Speed and accuracy ruled the day.

When I come to one of my franchises today, I often drive up in a beat-up Honda, wearing workout clothes. I had one employee tell me that he expected me to be in a Mercedes, wearing a suit and tie. "Why do you dress so casually?" he asked me. His tone implied that he was incredulous seeing me looking so down-to-earth every day, which defied his expectations. But the message I'm trying to convey is I'm hardworking, just like you, and no different. Hence, owners have no special prerogatives and operate no differently from their employees. Owners have to stay on top of the details and work hard, just like their staffers. I have to show up on time, do the job, and do it well, and if you do that, you'll be rewarded, too. I felt as if I had come a long way from owning the fitness center where I was just striving to get through the day and add new members. I was trying to let my employees know that we were in this together, which is why I'd clean up if something got spilled, fill in and make the doughnuts, fill the coffee filter—whatever needed to be done, I did the work, just as they did.

And one of the things I do is try to be a role model. So when I arrive at a Dunkin' franchise and see Heather, a regular customer, I'll ask her, "How's your grandma doing? Is she any better?" I've gotten to know Heather, and my identifying her makes her feel special and shows what happens when customers create a relationship with the franchise. I'm also letting my employees know that bonding with our clientele is the way to go.

I was modeling my behavior on what I wanted them to do. Do whatever job is needed. Look at the whole picture. Build relationships. I'd often talk with the staff about what it was like for me starting out, what I learned, how I tried to observe and take in everything. I was aiming to become their role model without having to state that I was. The proof was in the doing.

HIRING THE STAFF WITH THE RIGHT QUALITIES IS CRUCIAL

Not all staff are able to develop a rapport with the customers. It all depends on hiring the right staff, and that's one of the trickiest assignments a franchise owner contends with. What I learned early on was that people will look good based on their résumés. But résumés don't tell the whole story, and indeed, they reveal only a fraction of the full picture.

One of the key things I look for when I scrutinize a résumé is continuity. I avoid hiring what I call "hoppers." Those are the people who spend six months at McDonald's, then jump to Burger King for six months, go on to Arby's, move to a Buffalo Wild Wings, and then seek employment at Dunkin. Often a $1 an hour raise will lure them, with ease. Why work for $12 an hour when you can make $13 an hour, so they hop to the next chain. The way I saw it, they could build a better tomorrow staying with me, developing new skills, and getting on a track to become assistant manager, rather than jumping ship for an extra $25 a month. Looking at things from the long-haul perspective sometimes paid off beyond the immediate paycheck.

For many entry-level employees, the grass is perceived as always greener someplace else. Every restaurant chain has its strengths and limitations, but some employees think jumping from one chain to the other will be advantageous. But not for me. I won't hire them. Mostly because based on past performance, they won't stay; they'll just look to jump ship six months later no matter how well I treat them or how personable I am.

As I noted earlier in the book, what I do is ask them a series of questions to ascertain their character and their long-term goals to determine if they're right for my Dunkin' outlet. "Where do you want to be one year from today? Five years? Ten years?" If they say they'd like to be a shift leader or manager, I know this person is likely a right fit. As I also recounted earlier, one future employee told me that he expected to own his own franchise in a year. That person was rejected. "Too unrealistic and thinks too much of himself," I thought.

I'm looking for several traits that will lead to success at a Dunkin'. One is an ability to stay calm. Customers can fly off the handle at any moment. I've been cursed at, spit at, belittled, and worse. But any employee who curses back at the customers exacerbates the situation. Staying composed and settled when things get riled up is the best way to defuse the situation. So I seek out employees who can maintain their composure amid any growing chaos. Sometimes during the interview, I'd challenge some statement the interviewees made, just to test them to see how they'd react. Did they get defensive? Stay calm? Could they maintain their viewpoint without getting their back up? I tried to create a situation that would test their emotional reaction to being pressured as much as I could.

At the risk of sounding simplistic, I'm looking for employees who can smile, look customers in the eye, make contact with them easily, and build rapport. Nobody knows what kind of day someone is having. Sometimes the genuine smile at the drive-through might be the saving grace for someone who is having a really bad morning. A hardened, grizzled look and a frown just don't set the right tone at Dunkin'.

I also look for people who can multitask. As an employee is pouring iced coffee, another customer jumps up to order an egg sandwich, while a mother comes up to the counter to ask for a rag because her son has dirtied up the floor. Everything happens at once, so employees who can juggle several balls in the air perform the best. Methodical, slow-moving employees who can handle only one thing at a time and get bent out of shape when asked to perform two things at once will founder at Dunkin'. Hence, I pursue multitaskers who can stay calm in the maddening frenzy of a fast-food eatery. In our industry, the manager is often the first line of defense against impending chaos.

Because so many things need to be done at once—working with a colleague, dealing with customers, keeping an eye on guests coming into the store, keeping the drive-through line moving—multitasking has become one of the key skills required. The days of poring over one activity for a sustained period are over.

I'm also a major advocate of people gaining a second chance. I've hired ex-felons, and in my view, once they've paid their debt to society, they have a clean slate. If they can prove that they're honest and reliable, I'll give them a chance of doing well. And in my experience, most thrive. I've hired employees who had rap sheets dating back to age 16 with convictions related to drugs or a gun, but in prison, they took courses, and they express remorse about their mistakes. Here's what I tell them: "I don't judge you.

Just show up on time and do your job and follow our directions and you'll do well."

Hiring "newbies," those who have never toiled at a fast-food eatery, is often the best sales associate or cashier to hire. They have no bad habits to break, they are often teachable, and you get to train them in what your expectations are and how to meet them. Give me a newbie every time.

Therefore, think about how much specializing the job requires and whether or not you have the time to train the person. These things matter when deciding how much experience your hires need before starting a job. In most cases, starting your training with a clean slate might seem slow at first, but ultimately it's more efficient and effective than having to wipe the hard drive clean and reprogramming it. Character is key when hiring. If the person is focused and teachable, the potential for that hire to learn quickly and the right way as well as grow into other areas of the job is optimal.

When I hire people, I'm immediately thinking about how to retain them. I want employees to stay for the long haul, and the best way to achieve that is to train them right. The more I can inculcate the Dunkin' way of doing things, blended in with the Yonas way of operating, the better chance I have of holding on to them for the long haul. When I ask cashiers why they leave after two or three months, the usual response I get is "They threw me into the fire. I couldn't keep up. I had two orders at the drive-through, guests inside, and mobile apps, and it was all coming at me at once." We need to train staff to slow down, multitask, ask for help, and not take things personally, and if they can do that, they stay. I constantly point out to new employees the success stories of staff who have moved up. I cite Shannon, our multiunit manager, who started as a cashier, became shift leader, always showed up on time, proved reliable, and expressed an interest to move up and stay with Dunkin'. She became my spokesperson for what it takes to advance at a fast-food chain like Dunkin'. Turnover is the bane of most businesses' existence, requiring considerable time to find the right people, then train them, then break them in, and then familiarize them with your culture.

But the major reason why people leave Dunkin', not to mention most other fast-food eateries and other jobs as well, stems from problems with their boss. The most common refrain that I've heard in the restaurant business is "My boss didn't treat me right. He (or she) had a short fuse, criticized me for little mistakes, never complimented me, and didn't appreciate me." The lack of recognition hurts most Dunkin' employees who want to be appreciated for working hard and dealing with conflict and sometimes rude customer behavior.

What I preach to my managers is the mantra "Make work fun." If staff members are enjoying their team, coming to work each day with bounce in their step, rather than feeling maligned and aggrieved, they'll stay. Even if another chain offers them $1 more per hour, they'll ask for a raise in order to stay. But if they feel begrudged and overwhelmed and underappreciated, they'll leap across town for the next dollar raise.

BUILD A CAREER PATH TO MOVE YOUR TALENTED STAFF UP THE LADDER

The other factor that comes into play about retaining staff is moving them up the career path. When the cashier becomes shift leader, and then assistant manager, and strives to become manager, then staff stay on the job and feel no reason to wander.

What I aimed to do at every franchise I owned was to create an independent culture, "Yonas's culture," while I adhered to Dunkin's protocols. When I was starting out in my entry-level jobs at Burger King, my managers, David, Laura, and Moses, made working there fun, even while it was still hard work. We enjoyed each other's company and laughed and conveyed a strong sense of energy. We weren't going through the motions; we genuinely enjoyed working there. It felt like a family. That's the goal I've been trying to create at every restaurant I've owned, both franchises and, later, independents.

FOR EXPANDING YOUR BUSINESS

TIP #1
Early on, Seek out Friends and Family Who Can Become Key Investors

You don't need to have $325,000 (or more) in your bank account to open a franchise. But you do need to raise money from trusted friends and family members who are looking to increase their investments. Start thinking about whom you can tap as you begin the franchise process.

TIP #2
Gain Operating Experience

If you're interested in pursuing franchise experience, learn how the restaurant works from every possible angle: working in the kitchen, ordering food, dealing with the chef, handling customers, taking care of the front of the house, reading social media feedback on Yelp, dealing with customer complaints. The more you know, the better equipped you'll be to handle future issues.

TIP #3
Learn How to Treat the Customers

Pleasing the customers and retaining them are keys to restaurant success. Without the customers, you're just a place with tables and chairs. Focus on the customers. Make them happy. Be accurate in delivering orders. Keep the food fresh.

TIP #4
Hire the Right People, Reward Them, and Treat Them Right

Just like a Hollywood director needs to cast the right actors to make the film sizzle, so is a franchisee required to choose the right employees to ensure that the restaurant operates on all cylinders. Know exactly what qualities you want, and aim to hire people with those qualities. Point out what they're doing right, and make course corrections when they lapse into mistakes. But always treat them with respect.

TIP #5
Don't Scrimp

Restaurant franchises need to be upgraded. Equipment must be kept new. And the more equipment you have, the more efficient your staff will be. Investing in new espresso machines and blenders, for example, pays off in quicker service.

TIP #6
Learn from the Masters

My attitude was that franchise owners are the experts. They know what they're doing. They've been operating Dunkin's since they first debuted in Quincy, Massachusetts, in 1950, so that's over 70 years of success. How could I possibly know more than they do? When I overheard a franchisee suggest that he knew more than they did, I figured that this operator should launch his own business since he can't play by the franchisee's rules. To me, he was like a fish out of water. My outlook was if we follow these steps, we can be successful. Why mess with success?

TIP #7
Target Your Customers

During the training, I also realized something significant about who Dunkin's target customers were and how they compared with Starbucks's clientele. Dunkin' was a blue-collar place. It was where the landscapers, construction crews, and utility workers traveled most days to jump-start their day with a cup of joe and a breakfast sandwich. Starbucks tended to attract the hipper, younger, cooler audience. And I also give Starbucks people credit because they were constantly innovating, and I felt that Dunkin' could learn from them. That pumpkin latte was a hit, and we learned to adapt it to our audience as well.

And when the Starbucks folks introduced their app for quick mobile ordering, I knew it would only be a matter of time before Dunkin' followed in their footsteps. Sometimes when you can't be the leader, coming in a close second is noteworthy.

I had done my homework and read about Dunkin's relationships with franchisees, and there were some problems in its history. Several franchisees had fudged their reported sales, falsifying figures, causing Dunkin' to sue them. Their royalties were based on paying Dunkin' a percentage of sales, so by withholding the full numbers, they were making more money for themselves. I said to myself early on that I would be honest and avoid all problems. By that time, Dunkin' had updated its system, so cheating was much more difficult anyway.

TIP #8
Know When to Go Beyond Franchise Protocols

When you're franchising, you're signing up to run a proven system guided by Dunkin's procedures and guidelines. And why mess with the company's success? Just the same, though, as big as Dunkin' is, it doesn't know it all. And that means sometimes you have to adjust the methods, introduce some new ones, and test out something that doesn't quite fit into the company's marketing strategies—without deviating too much from standard procedure.

TIP #9
Introduce Your Own Approaches

At our local Dunkin' outlet, we started selling Dunkin's maple bacon doughnut.

We started selling Dunkin's maple donuts, but we added something to them that Midwesterners loved: a bacon taste. We called them maple bacon donuts, and they were sweet, salty, and irresistible.

We started making 10 dozen of them and sold out in a half hour. We couldn't keep them in the store. Then we made a hundred dozen of them, and they sold out in hours. But they were so labor intensive to make, and required the output of so many staff members, that we discontinued them. It took too much out of the staff. We also got some complaints from other Dunkin' franchisees who were dealing with customer disappointment when customers ordered them in other areas of Illinois. And when we suggested to the parent franchise that the doughnuts should be made available in Chicago, the company felt strongly that they wouldn't thrive in Chicago, the nexus of its sales, where too many guests were weight conscious. So the point is, it's fine to experiment, but even innovation has its limitations.

TIP #10
Give Back to the Community

I emphasized becoming part of the community and giving back. For example, when we opened our first Dunkin' in 2013, it was only about 30 minutes from a town called Washington, Illinois, where a tornado hit in November of that year, devastating the town. We brought coffee and doughnuts to dish out to first responders for weeks as a way of showing faith in the community. We sent out no press releases and didn't do any media, which is how I wanted it. We did it as a way of giving back to the community, not as a publicity ploy.

But weeks afterward, neighbors would send cards and letters to thank us for giving out so many freebies to first responders. They knew, they let their friends know, and our business started getting stronger post-disaster. I think our commitment to the community played a role in our resurgence, and it's been a core belief of running a franchise wherever it is located.

TIP #11
Master the Art of Upselling

I've trained my staff to be personable, upbeat, and positive, and that sets the tone for upselling. That is selling clients just a little more than they ordered. If we can catch the customers in the right mood and frame of mind, suggesting they add hash browns to their egg sandwich boosts the check 15 percent or so. Add that up over the course of a day, and revenue expands by 15 percent, and that helps the bottom line. So if Alan, the sales associate, is personable or has developed a rapport with the customer, the customer often doesn't want to disappoint Alan and will agree. It's all about establishing trust with the customer, which leads to upselling, which increases our sales by a healthy 15 percent or so.

TIP #12
Focus on Motivating Your Employees

If we motivate employees to upsell, it pays off. Some call this technique "incentivizing" employees. I give out bonuses for staff who boost sales more than others, and sometimes I distribute gift cards so the whole team can have some free snacks or dinner. And for many of our younger employees, the ones who are 16 or 17, what often works best is ordering in pizza for dinner for the staff who boosted sales the most. Give them a goal, and let them hit it, and they feel special. And when you treat them to dinner, the pizza tastes so much better. Food always tastes better when someone else is buying. No matter what, incorporating upselling in a natural way, without being pushy and turning customers off, is critical to increasing sales on a daily basis.

TIP #13
Offering Special Deals Can Boost Business

I've preached to my staff that following the Dunkin' guidelines make the most sense and enables each location to be successful. And I firmly believe in that approach. But sometimes innovating and going beyond the established protocol makes good business sense. For example, many of the local supermarket chains such as Kroger and Jewel have had great success with discounting coupons. Why don't we try that at Dunkin'? The parent franchise didn't think it worked, but we experimented with "Buy a dozen, get the next dozen half-price off" and "Buy a large coffee and get a small coffee at half price for your next purchase." All these deals resonated with guests, despite the fact that headquarters resisted.

CHAPTER 6

WHEN TOUGH TIMES HAPPEN

Growth, Scaling, and the Ultimate Balancing Act

There hopefully comes a time when your business is in motion, you have a team you trust, you have experimented and pivoted, and you are reporting financial growth. What's next? For some this is enough, and very much a feather in their cap, as we all know what the statistics are for starting, operating, and sustaining small businesses. But let's face it; the entrepreneurial spirit is by its nature serial. Once we get a taste of success and we feel confident and comfortable in our roles, and of course have some extra capital (finally!), expansion starts to tickle our brains.

What you'll be learning in this chapter is how to get a new business off the ground, getting it up and running and succeeding from opening day. Here's the research and homework and hiring practices that it takes to overcome the odds and flourish, whether it's a franchise restaurant, kayak business, app, food truck, secondhand clothing store, or dating service.

And then after the first venture is showing signs of success, there are some entrepreneurs who have a yearning inside them to keep going and open a second and then a third. And frankly, the way franchises are arranged, opening up one won't sustain a healthy enough living for many an entrepreneur. Owning multiple franchises, once you recognize what works and how to be profitable, is the easiest way to generate steady cash.

Growth can come in any direction to the entrepreneur who is looking for expansion. Some entrepreneurs have had success with opening trendy hair salons, and there are wellness franchises, fix-it electronic gadget franchises, healing centers, and pet walking businesses.

When my partners, Ron and Michael, and I signed the deal to open our initial Dunkin' Donuts franchise in 2013, we intended from the outset to expand. Our initial deal was a one-plus-two agreement.

With these franchise agreements, common with many brands, the entrepreneur signs a three-store deal, by opening one location and having two others protected in designated territories. So that sets up the entrepreneurs for future growth, but you don't pay any additional money until you're ready to expand, though usually there's a several-year agreement that forces you to act within a certain time period. The partnership helps both the franchise and the operator, because both are looking to own multiple locations, which yields continuity for the restaurant brand and, ideally, steady, increased income for the expanding franchisee.

Hence, we'd open up one Dunkin' Donuts franchise and then move as quickly as possible adding our second and our third. My dream of entrepreneurship was turning into a reality, doughnut by doughnut and one coffee with milk and two sugars at a time.

From our point of view, opening up more than one location enabled us to withstand any downturns or revenue setbacks. For example, our second franchise in Pekin, Illinois, was near Illinois Central College, so once the semester ended, our revenue decreased by 30 percent or so. Once we owned two franchises, though, if one was prospering and the other was facing a slow-down, revenue stabilized between the two.

Owning multiple eateries, or several businesses, was one of the key ways to weather most economic downturns. So if the location in Normal had to shut down for a brief time during construction, the Pekin franchise would be generating income; this way revenue could be sustained, and we could make payroll. In my view, the more outlets we owned, the more it would spread revenue around and enable us to endure any pullback due not only to inclement weather but to any other setback.

Once we owned franchises in Florida, that really benefited us and enabled us to withstand snowstorms in Illinois, because the sun was shining in Tampa and smoothie sales there were good.

When we signed the Dunkin' Donuts deal, it awarded us franchises within a certain designated area in central Illinois between Bloomington and Peoria. Headquarters at Dunkin' Donuts assigns the area, taking into account where the other franchises are situated to avoid stealing sales from existing franchisees. So it's walking a thin line of expanding sales in a certain locale without reducing revenue from the already-operating locations. But we trusted that the company knew the best locations, where a new franchisee could thrive without encroaching on previous outposts.

In retrospect, many current franchisees feel threatened when a new outlet opens within several miles of them. Will sales be cannibalized? Will it hurt our sales? Those are normal questions to ask.

Staffing issues were also improved once we opened the second franchise. If someone called in sick at the Normal location, we could transfer over a cashier from the Pekin location, and everything flowed smoothly.

When it comes to capitalizing a second franchise, many outsiders look at the $40,000 royalty fee paid to the franchise as one guiding figure. But that entails a fraction of how much money is actually required to open a second franchise. In our case, we acquired the land in Pekin for about $250,000, remodeled it for $450,000, and all told needed about a $1 million to open.

This meant for us as owners and operators that we were turning into real estate owners, not only franchise owners. And that brought us into another realm. Even if that Dunkin' franchise floundered, we could extricate ourselves from the franchise agreement, demolish the building, and turn the land into something else. A strip mall? A commercial business? A small apartment building? You name it. We weren't just restaurateurs; we were landlords and landowners, and that lifted us up and gave us various options for the future. It also could lead to passive income, where you receive steady income or rent from your tenant without having to toil those 12- to 14-hour days.

To raise the $1 million, we took out loans from banks for about half that amount, an SBA 504 loan for about 35 percent of the cost, and invested about 15 percent of our money. Because we were turning our first franchise around and boosting revenue (more about that soon), we used the cash flow from our profits to provide the $150,000 of our own money. I continued with the same two partners to finance the second franchise.

At our first Dunkin' Donuts, we were facing management issues. As noted in an earlier chapter, the manager we selected made life difficult for our employees, and when your staff is unhappy and clashing with the boss, revenue is going to fall, and customers aren't going to be happy. We resolved to fix that, which led to the manager being dismissed.

Since we had borrowed close to a million dollars to develop the first franchise and then tagged on a second million dollars to finance the second one, you might think that we were burdening ourselves with undue pressure and too much debt. But there was one critical factor that mitigated our borrowing: We were securing these loans with real estate. Since we were buying the land on which we built the two Dunkin' Donuts franchises, it alleviated some of our concern.

Real estate values, except on rare occasions, inevitably rise. So if the Dunkin' franchise faltered, and we had to sell, at least the value of the land would escalate and would lessen the risk entailed with borrowing money. And that was only one factor that lessened the debt risk. So we were not only in the franchise business; we were in real estate.

Another prevailing factor was that Dunkin' Donuts was a national brand that elicited strong customer awareness. When in doubt, many customers go with what they know, and most of our customers were reared on Dunkin's coffee, doughnuts, and egg sandwiches. And Dunkin' did national advertising to build brand awareness and sustain its image. Could a Dunkin' fail? Of course it could, but we were betting on name recognition, a solid product, and a strong team.

In my 12 years working with Dunkin', it was extremely rare to hear of any that closed and went under, though I'm sure it happens. But it's an anomaly. Dunkin' does everything it can to ensure that each franchise is successful, and that starts with choosing the right location. And then, as described earlier in the book, its intensive, thorough, and lengthy interview process lessens the chances that some unprepared owner would take over the keys and launch the business. The company's goal is to limit the risk of failure and maximize the chance of success.

What's the takeaway for businesses starting out that aren't restaurant franchises? Just as Dunkin' encourages every future operator to do his or her homework, become familiar with the brand, and study the operating principles, new owners must do their own due diligence. In order to stay one step ahead of the competition, owners must know which customers they're targeting, know how to reach them, understand their competitors, and devise an edge that will lure customers to the new business, whether it is e-commerce, a recycling plant, or a kayak company. Staying one step ahead is critical to success.

Was I terrified, deep down inside, about borrowing so much money? You bet I was. At the beginning we had to fire the manager and report fluctuations in revenue. I worried. But I always felt that failure wasn't an option. What was driving me was my need to succeed, my desire to be self-employed and avoid becoming a corporate employee, dependent on the whims of the boss.

In fact, at the outset, I was working 18-hour shifts and more at the original Dunkin'. And that left little time for sleeping. We baked the doughnuts through the night, so I'd start my shift at 4 p.m. and work through until 11 a.m. the next day. I called my approach "tunnel vision." Nothing was going to stop me from making this first Dunkin' a success. If we could hit a home run with the first one, it would lead to stronger chances of making the second and third ones that we had signed up for a success. If I had to sleep only five hours a night, so be it. I felt as if I didn't have much of a choice. If I wanted to ensure that this Dunkin' outlet was going to flourish, I had to do everything in my power to make it so. It took hard work, commitment, minimal sleep, and total concentration, and when we made mistakes, which we were bound to make, we fixed them as quickly as possible.

This is one difference between being an entrepreneur and working for someone else. When you work for yourself, you never turn the business off. It's always with you. Never clocking out. You work it during the day, think about it on the way home, talk about it at the dinner table, and sometimes toss and turn in your sleep, though you can devise clever solutions at that time.

How do fledgling entrepreneurs establish any semblance of work-life balance when their startup business is all-consuming? Every new owner has to answer that question individually. As for me, the fitness center was my saving grace. It kept me sane. I was hanging out with friends, and luckily, we'd talk about many things that would enable me to get a respite from my all-devouring startup. And working out was also a welcome breath of fresh air. No one was on my case, asking me for skimmed milk, not regular milk. But for another entrepreneur, it could be playing bridge online, or playing poker in person, or Rollerblading on a street. Choose your own diversion, but you will need some outlet to break the pressure.

We needed to fix several things to ensure our first Dunkin' was running efficiently and generating sufficient profits. As with launching any business, we faced some setbacks and disruptions in our first year. For example, my major miscue was in hiring the wrong manager. And it took me some time to evaluate what she was doing wrong, where she went awry, and what I had to do to remedy the situation.

Then we employed several of Dunkin's new marketing concepts to jump-start sales. For example, Dunkin's "Happy Hour," where guests could buy iced coffee for 99 cents from 2 p.m. to 6 p.m., proved to be a winner and crowd-pleaser. We let everyone know via discounted coupons mailed to their home address, and we posted the news on various Dunkin' Donut social media sites and our own social media pages. Since our second location was close to Illinois Central College, and students are often on a tight budget, business boomed.

Every business owner has to be inventive, timely, and ingenious to introduce a marketing concept that boosts revenue that works with the clientele. For example, in my independent eateries, Dakotas, business was sluggish in the winter when cold weather and snow discouraged visits downtown. Our patrons in 2022 were also contending with rising inflation and a recession. So what we did was to create value to lure in a crowd. We slashed the price of our core burger to $7, making a full dinner with a beverage easily attainable for under $20. People still wanted to dine out and meet friends, so our goal was to make it affordable. We were aiming to appeal to a wide range of people, not just a select few.

It's a lesson other entrepreneurs can draw from. If you own a dry-cleaning store, cut the prices from $5 a shirt to $4 and see what happens. If it's a mailbox business, cut the monthly price and market it.

And nowadays with targeted marketing on Facebook and other social media sites, you can target clients in your neighboring zip codes, or single women, or seniors—you name it.

At the same time, I trained my staff to upsell and entice guests with a second purchase. Staff were guided to ask customers, now saving a buck with the coupon for the iced coffee, if they wanted a doughnut, bagel sandwich, or hash browns, which could bring the check to $3 a person or more. In fact, I scrutinized sales and saw that every iced-coffee discount buyer was spending $3.50 per check, so it became a win-win. Lure them in, and encourage them to spend more.

And our customers were overjoyed that they didn't have to drive an extra 15 or 20 minutes into Peoria, the larger nearby city, for their daily cup of java and a doughnut. Happy customers return, which is what most of them were doing, and our cash register kept ringing away with sales. It became the go-to breakfast spot for many citizens of Normal.

Seeing how popular it was, we extended the hours until 7 p.m. The important thing was to attract college kids, make them feel at home, sell them something else, and keep them coming. Dunkin' was becoming a habit.

Our clientele at the Pekin outlet differed from the classic audience we attracted in Normal. In Pekin, it was mostly blue-collar workers who toiled at Caterpillar and the chemical plants, whereas Normal was predominantly a college town. Often they would fill up their cars at a gas station, buy a soda pop, and then come to us for a doughnut. If we could lure them into buying a Dunkin' coffee, we could save them a trip (at times), enhance our sales, and make them happy.

When I opened the second franchise, I kept my hiring moderate because I had faced some payroll issues and had a too-high payroll at the first outlet, and as stated previously, I was always aiming to keep my breakeven point low to ensure steady profits.

Owners learn from experience. In many ways, I found it much easier operating the second Dunkin' Donuts compared with the first. I knew more about the day-to-day running, filling customers' needs, knowing what would sell, ordering the right inventory, and converting more of our customers to beverage drinkers of latte and coffees, not just doughnut eaters.

Everyone loves a discount. The more we offered cut-rate deals, the more sales skyrocketed. We'd offer "Buy one large coffee, and get a small coffee at half price," and that was a crowd-pleaser. "Buy two croissants for $5 and get a medium coffee for 50 cents off" was another bargain that consumers dove into.

The more I could hook our customers on coffee, a high-margin item, the more our profits accelerated and our customer retention rate increased. Everyone likes value packages; particularly the offspring of parents from the Depression, who were raised to scrimp and save, couldn't resist the deals. And so did college students who were on a tight budget. And retirees. Nearly everyone loves a deal on breakfast or lunch or snacks.

And revenue started to climb. At first we did only $15,000 a week, and then when we started to introduce the discount, sales skyrocketed to $20,000 a week, then $25,000, and then $30,000; and finally sales settled in at $50,000 a week or over $2 million a year. We had turned a sluggish Dunkin' Donuts into a perennial favorite.

Another thing I noticed when we opened the second store was that I was spending much less time on the first. It reminded me of what happened in my own family when my daughter was born and my son was no longer an only child. All the attention gravitated to the baby, and my son felt slighted and overlooked. Focusing nearly all our attention on the second Dunkin' Donuts store to make sure it was successful had repercussions, although they were not dire. It was a cautionary tale, underscoring that I had to make sure revenue was flowing at both stores, not just the newest one.

TIME MANAGEMENT AND SELF-CARE

Running two stores, rather than one, could be overwhelming at first. And I'd be the first person to admit it. There were times that I struggled, feeling swamped and not in control. Luckily for

me, I was mentored by Jeff Wampler, a Dunkin' Donuts operational manager, who took me under his wing when he saw I was
struggling at first. That was when the original manager was losing control of her staff and revenue faltered. Wampler was a former Burger King employee like me, which bonded us forever. He
respected me and wanted me to do well.

Wampler also knew that I was a former soldier who possessed a thick-skin mentality. Really, he showed me tough love
because he was straight with me, didn't sugarcoat issues, and yet
suggested ways to correct what was going awry.

When the second store struggled for a while, he, first of all,
cautioned me not to open the third Dunkin' before we fixed the
problems of the second. Then he had me analyze hour by hour
where the revenue at the Dunkin's location in Normal was emanating from. At the beginning, because there were so many college
students in our audience, I figured that the lunch trade would drive
business. But when I analyzed the data, I learned that breakfast
sales from 5 a.m. to 11 a.m. were the dominant revenue source.

Since sales were so much higher during breakfast than lunch,
I put more emphasis on the morning hours and quickened the
time spent on the drive-through line, and revenue started to
expand. We also spent more time on training employees to ensure
quick service, and let the restaurant manager set the tone and set
the staff's direction. Sales started to shoot up, and we were on
our way to success.

I also readjusted my staff accordingly. I like to say that "I put
my aces in the right places." By that I mean my most talented,
resourceful employees were assigned the morning shift, and those
who weren't quite stellar were relegated to the afternoon shift
when business trailed off.

We also focused on speed, speed, speed. If we could get customers through that Dunkin's line in five minutes, not eight min-

utes, they were more likely to choose us over Starbucks. Rapid service in the morning, when everyone is super busy and off to work, matters greatly and can boost revenue and retain customers. We'd always bake a sufficient number of doughnuts and make sure the breakfast sandwiches were flowing.

At one point, when the numbers were down, Wampler said to me, "Yonas, are you still sure restaurant franchising is the career you really want, or do you think returning to corporate life may be best for you?" Maybe it was my military background, or maybe it was my upbringing at the Sudanese refugee camp, but I reacted the way I always did when the going got tough, when my back was against the wall, when times were tough, I dug down deep inside and told him that nothing was going to stop me now. This is what I was born to do, and we're going to fix it and get that franchise back to operating like a well-oiled machine.

What I learned most of all was that hiring the right managers played a critical role, training the staff was crucial, providing them with the best resources was vital, and investing in equipment was also essential—and all contributed to paying off long term. If you're operating a one-person business, you don't have to worry about recruiting managers, but you do have to build in the right resources and do your homework. And if your business is growing, hiring a manager with the requisite skills that fit your business, and the temperament that blends with your clientele, goes a long way to success.

Then at a conference I met a Dunkin' Donuts franchisee named Frank, who owned over 30 outlets. I figured I could learn something from his experience. "What's the key thing you've learned from owning multiple units?" I asked him.

"Learn how to trust your people and allow them to fail at times, and then correct them," he responded. "Everyone fails. You need to give them some slack. Don't micromanage them.

Give them room to fail and grow. I can't sit there and look over their shoulder and coddle them. Treat them like adults, not teenagers." Gleaning knowledge from Frank, I opted not to micromanage, and if a manager failed at some test, we'd discuss it, make adjustments, and move on.

I learned two major factors from owning two restaurant franchises. There are two major costs that we could control: food costs and labor costs. The rent or mortgage was fixed, as were utility fees. But if I could get a handle on keeping my food costs down, hiring the right number of managers, and not overhiring, I would more likely run a smooth-functioning organization.

And one more thing: No one ever discusses equipment maintenance, but it is the most overlooked cost. I knew the espresso and latte machines at some point were going to malfunction. Paint jobs were necessary. New equipment had to be bought. And so when the heating and air-conditioning system broke down, I invested $1,500 to buy a new unit, and the restaurant continued to operate effectively. It cost us money short term, but saved spending over the long haul, because older heating and cooling systems do break down and need to be fixed, and that slows business down while having to pay contractors to fix them. Long term, we saved by investing in new equipment.

Then I started introducing guerrilla marketing, the same marketing I did when I first opened Anytime Fitness. We always had a lot of food waste at each Dunkin', for example, doughnuts that didn't sell at the end of the day that we had to discard. But I figured I could turn our excess doughnuts into a winner. When I'd learn about local baseball Little Leagues, I brought over doughnuts for everyone and containers of coffee for the grown-ups and distributed them free, with some coupons for follow-up purchases. I'd do the same at local high school football games, and people in these small cities began to notice me. They'd know me as a Purple Heart winner, a military veteran, and a franchise owner who was involved in their communities. It spread the good word and boosted our business, and our local Dunkin's became known.

One customer once said to me, "Your Dunkin' feels like a mom-and-pop doughnut shop." And for me that was a very high compliment. We had the products that Dunkin' offered and the name recognition, but in Normal and Pekin, guests knew they were walking into Yonas's Dunkin' shops. It was as if I were branding my shops with my name on top of the national brand.

And remember we were all coming out of a recession that rocked the country in 2008. Consumers were still seeking value, looking to stretch their dollars, and those 99-cent iced coffees and discounted coupons resonated for many of them.

And then my partners and I opened our third Dunkin' Donuts outlet in Washington, Illinois, a suburb of Peoria, so we kept all the franchises in relative proximity to one another. Washington is near Eureka, the town where Ronald Reagan attended college. Washington has a small-town, country feel, exemplified by my plumber (from Eureka), who was a member of a church that started buying dozens of doughnuts from us on Sundays. It felt as if everyone knew each other in Washington and Eureka.

The more popular our Dunkin' Donuts was getting, the more I reached out to the community. I liked what the Special Olympics stood for and started fundraising for it. I didn't take out any ads about our donating to the Special Olympics, or call attention to any other charitable deed, but let each deed speak for itself. And people in those communities knew which bosses gave back and which turned away. And since I was one of the few Black franchise owners, and was someone with a military record and a Purple Heart, I also stood out. It felt as if everyone in those three towns knew who Yonas was and how he owned those Dunkin' Donuts in town.

But when the first Dunkin' Donuts was struggling, and I was finding ways to increase the revenue and cut my costs, I feared that I could drown with debt and would be unable to pay my bills. In short, I was panicking. I started thinking of ways to create a new revenue flow, based on some skills that I acquired in the military.

Even though I was committed to making this franchise work, you never know when times can go bad, a recession can linger, and a doughnut franchise runs into a roadblock. When I was in the Army, one of the key skills I learned was how to make guns. And not knowing if this Dunkin' Donuts venture was going to fly, I applied for a Federal Firearms License. To get the license, I had to discuss my expertise and undergo a background check. Once I received the go-ahead to get a license and start building guns, I had to meet with the chief of police in Yorkville to discuss my plans.

I named my company "Civilian Force Arms," which sounded very official and very police-oriented. I started making AR-47 rifles in my basement. I tinkered with the formula that I was taught and tried to improve the guns. I started selling them at the SHOT (the Shooting, Hunting, and Outdoor Trade Show) held annually in Las Vegas.

Civilian Force Arms started garnering a national reputation, and I became known as one of the first Black-owned manufacturers of guns. I was doing so well that I moved the manufacturing out of my basement and into a warehouse. But just as sales started to spike, the Dunkin' franchises were turning around and generating lots of cash. I sold the gun company to an Arizona-based entrepreneur who moved it there. Every now and then, I think about, somewhere in retirement, returning to the trade and manufacturing $10,000 state-of-the-art AR-47 rifles.

Since the Dunkin' franchises were starting to take off, we were looking to expand. When we capitalized the third one in

Washington, which cost more money because of additional construction fees, at about $1.3 million, we were now borrowing in excess of $3 million for the three locations. And while it still could be considered a precarious venture, the risks were minimized since real estate values almost always rise. The real estate values of the land we owned for the first two Dunkin's now exceeded $2 million. If we encountered a major setback, we could sell the land and eradicate our debt.

Our cash flow had risen at the three stores, so that we were generating enough cash to pay our mortgage with ease and save money. Hence, the new debt didn't feel as if it was a weight on our shoulders, as we were generating over a million dollar in sales in the two existing franchises. Covering our debt was the cost of doing business. By March 2015, just two years after we opened our first Dunkin', we had three flourishing outlets.

The more stores you open, the better you get at running them, and the fewer headaches you have. I was told by Dunkin' executives that they considered me a superstar, that I had built and operated three thriving stores by boosting revenue, and I was known and respected by the community. I felt as if there was no stopping me and that there wasn't anything I couldn't accomplish.

Feedback in all forms is important. Of course, great feedback like I had received kept the fire inside me nice and stoked. But seeking out feedback can also help you define the dim spots and help you see the realities that need tending to be addressed and fixed. I've always seen feedback as just taking in new information: Praise is helpful because it says you're doing a good job, and constructive feedback is useful because it enables you to make adjustments.

Surveying your team—one way to get feedback—is an essential role of a leader. I found that many of my employees were my best advocates. They would state that I treated them well; that I wouldn't ask them to do anything that I wouldn't do; that I was in the trenches with them, making the coffee and cleaning up spills.

I also learned a considerable amount from dealing with the overall Dunkin' Donuts brand. The company achieved many things including launching a national marketing campaign that made Dunkin' a household name. And that kind of brand recognition is invaluable and incalculable. Everyone, so it seems, recognizes that Dunkin' means coffee and a doughnut, or coffee and an egg sandwich, breakfast or lunch, at a lower price than the more upscale Starbucks fare. Saving that 50 cents when you drink coffee once daily, or twice daily, carries a major savings for most working-class people who aren't Wall Street executives making six-figure salaries. And unexpectedly, we attract many of the affluent too who like the taste of the coffee or the lower prices or both.

Dunkin' also offered, at times, specific analytic assistance. If revenue was down, the company would offer numbers on speed of service with suggestions of how to step it up. If business rose at 8 a.m. but plateaued at 10 a.m., the company would make suggestions about what to do to boost revenue during slower times. But, ultimately, it was up to the franchisee to execute.

Dunkin' won't come in and pay your bills if your revenue dips or a recession starts. You are fully independent; it's your hard work and strategies that determine your success, and Dunkin' serves as the overlord.

When I look back on how quickly those three Dunkin' franchises became successful, I remember clearly one of the first days, around July 2013, when the first franchise was opening. I had gone to the bank to pick up loose change—change that wasn't rolled—and when I exited the bank, it was pouring outside. I took about two steps out the door, and the change bag ripped, and $100 in nickels, dimes, and quarters fell to the ground. I stooped down to pick up the change, and an affable woman beside me saw my distress and helped me reclaim the coins. I was soaked, as was she, but we picked up much of the $100 in change, and I returned to delivering it to the store.

Just three years before, I was starting out, drenched by the rain, and I had no idea if I would be a success or not. And three years later, I felt as if I had accomplished so much. The world was in front of me, waiting to be hatched. I was an immigrant, and I was fast becoming an entrepreneurial success story.

Now that my franchise business has expanded, I don't need to go pick up loose change anymore. Now feeling more confident, I'll ask the bank to roll my change, proving I've grown and can learn from my mistakes and accidents.

Key Tips

FOR TOUGH TIMES

TIP #1
Increase Your Debt Payments

It may not make sense to outsiders, but taking on more debt is the way to get rich. Unless you're born with a trust fund or silver spoon or have an inheritance, most entrepreneurs don't have an extra $1 million or so in their bank account. Hence, you have to take out loans via banks and SBA loans, or secure angel investors, or draw interest from a private equity firm. For us, SBA loans led to the banks, but the debt was necessary and manageable. It takes a certain mindset to go into debt, deepen it, and still have the confidence that the investments—the franchises—will prosper. I believe in my business models, the franchise brand, and our ability to generate business and please customers, so the debt was the necessary underpinning for us to raise capital.

Having close to $3 million in debt could unnerve anyone, but to me it was the cost of doing business. Since the real estate we bought was worth $2 million or more, it alleviated many of my fears.

TIP #2
You're Going to Fail at Certain Tasks

No one is perfect. You can't do everything right. For example, I hired a manager for the first Dunkin' franchise who didn't possess the requisite skills, failed to communicate with most of her staff, and alienated many of them, and yet I transferred her to another store. I couldn't accept that she was flunking, and it took me a long time to recognize that I chose the wrong person. Once I did, I had to dismiss her and select a replacement who had the right skills.

TIP #3
It's All About the Manager

Once you open up two franchises, you can't be at both places simultaneously. So the store manager assumes a more significant role than in the past. Owners have to train better, and choose leaders with the right skills to oversee the operation when you're called to the second franchise. Putting trust in the management team is critical to each location's success. Micromanaging won't work because it inhibits trust, and the leaders, feeling as if someone is looking over their shoulder, are stultified. Train well, choose staff with the requisite skills, and then let them flourish.

TIP #4
Create the Career Ladder

Retaining staff in the restaurant industry is one critical factor in success. I call many restaurant employees "hoppers" because they move from Arby's to Wendy's to White Castle to Dunkin' in pursuit of the $1 or $2 an hour raise. The way to keep people is to promote them. Train them with the necessary skills, and make them shift leader, assistant manager, and then unit manager, and finally give them a 5 percent ownership interest. That'll lead to keeping them and stopping the musical chairs.

TIP #5
Use Deals to Attract the Customers

The 99-cent iced coffee in the afternoon boosted our business. And once we attracted those customers, they could become regulars. I introduced a slew of deals to bring the customers in the door, and once in, found ways to welcome them, get to know them, and bring them back. What can you offer as a direct line to a new customer base? What can you add value to that you are already doing or selling?

Offering value and discounts worked for our target consumers. When times were bad, and Covid hit, or inflation rose, or gas prices went up, guests would cut back on their weekly trips. The working-class people who stopped in daily would find their way in three times a week instead of five, and that could reduce our revenue by 10 to 15 percent, and that hurt the bottom line.

That's when we'd step up our secret crowd booster: coupons. "Get a free coffee with your cup of coffee." "Iced tea for 99 cents," not $2. "Buy a large coffee and get a free donut." Once we hit those discount levers, guests would keep coming in for more because they got a deal they couldn't refuse.

TIP #6
Become Part of the Community

The more engaged I could become in the community, the more people would know about Yonas's Dunkin' Donuts. Many of them knew me, recognized that I raised money for charity, and felt I cared about the community. And that made it easier for them to return, to make our Dunkin' Donuts part of their breakfast or lunch routine. We weren't an anonymous national brand, but a local brand with an owner immersed in the community.

TIP #7
Encourage Your Staff to Become Advocates

The more the staff felt I was watching their backs, the better the eatery performed. They knew I'd take out the mop and clean up the coffee spill, just as they did. I'd clean the toilets, and I'd problem-solve if a customer found the coffee tepid and needed a new cup.

TIP #8
Treat Your Staff the Way You Want to Be Treated

I never felt better than my staff. We were all in this business together. Making fresh coffee and ensuring that the doughnuts were baked, the egg sandwiches were fresh, and the customers were happy, that was the role we all played.

Since each employee is different, what clicks with one person doesn't score with another. Getting to know each one better is critical to making a staff hum. If I knew that Robin was involved in her high school's cheerleading squad, I'd ask her how the game went on Saturday. Taking an interest, showing concern, treating her like an individual, not just a number, went a long way to building trust. I'm engaged with the employee and tried to show my interest. And it was authentic, because I cared about the employees and wanted what was best for them.

TIP #9
Train Your Managers to Listen and Act Accordingly

One of the critical messages that I conveyed to my managers, to ensure that my Dunkin' staff operated as a team, was that listening to their staff was paramount. If you listen carefully and attentively, your staff will convey the missing piece of the puzzle of what works optimally for them. More assignments? Added responsibilities? Later shifts? Ways to move up the corporate ladder? Bonuses? Recognition for a job well done? They'll reveal to you, either in a subtle way or explicitly, what they're looking for. If you listen well enough.

And what most often happens when I conduct exit interviews is that it's the manager's behavior that pushed the employees out the door. Not being respected, being talked down to, being belittled or slighted, not being recognized, not being given a raise, the reasons are manifold, but it is often the manager's behavior that drives the employees away rather than retains them. Hire the right managers, get them to treat employees right, customize their efforts toward employees, and you're three-quarters the way to operating a successful franchise.

Paying employees more boosts their morale. But money didn't solve all problems or satisfy all employees.

Some employees needed to be replaced. They were toxic, poisoned the atmosphere, and damaged teamwork and required a change of scenery. But most times, my goal was training staff, trusting them, building their careers, sharpening their skills, and having the managers work closely with them to increase the effectiveness of each store.

So making sure the staff was primed to work with customers, and ensuring my managers were leading and supporting them, those were my primary concerns.

TIP #10
Always Look for the Next Opportunity

When I owned the first Dunkin', I was thinking about where to open the second. When the second started to thrive, I focused on opening the third. I tried to be one step ahead at all times.

CHAPTER 7

YOU CAN'T BE IN TWO PLACES AT ONE TIME

Knowing How to Manage Multiple Businesses at Once

Once I co-owned and operated three Dunkin' Donuts, started building revenue at each outlet, and learned how to run a franchise effectively, I got into a groove. It's like a lightbulb went on and flashed the message, "You know how to do this." I felt as if I had gained a sense of mastery. I had gained the experience and savviness in how to run a franchised restaurant: knowing what works, what doesn't, how to manage a staff, how to work with my partners, how to develop rapport with clients, how to attract them and win them back, how to order food, how to service and keep up my equipment and physical space, and how to deal with the other franchise owners.

And the skills I had mastered in running a restaurant franchise will carry over to any other business: operating it, appealing to customers, managing and motivating a staff, and solving one problem after another.

Revenue at my three Dunkin' Donuts was accelerating. And the better they did, the happier Dunkin' executives were. My three Dunkin' outlets were scoring in the top five in Illinois outlets and hitting milestones such as higher average check per customer receipts, a criterion that Dunkin' headquarters and leadership took very seriously. The more revenue the locations generated, the more I thought about expanding outlets.

At the beginning, I'd run into a brick wall and feel overwhelmed or stymied. But now after running several Dunkin' outlets for over two years and juggling all of them at once, I felt more in control. A district manager once told me that the biggest leap involved moving from owning one Dunkin' to two, and he was right. You can't be in two places at one time, so you learn to delegate, and do so effectively.

But of all the skills I had to master in owning multiple franchises, the one that stood out by far was managing people. That was at the crux of making each eatery successful. Everyone assumes that restaurant franchises live or die with pleasing the customers, and there's a relative amount of truth there. But the real nexus of making the franchise hum and sizzle involves managing your staff. In my experience, dealing with customers is considerably easier, on the whole, than supervising and overseeing your employees.

Let's face it—most customers spend a limited amount of time at a restaurant franchise. These days with mobile app ordering and drive-throughs, it's quick, convenient, in and out. And even the few who dine in spend only about 20 minutes. That's why it's called "fast food." But employees are there for six to eight hours a shift, four or five days a week, on a continuing basis. That's where the real job gets done.

Financially, the more restaurant franchises I opened, the easier it seemed to get. One might assume that multiplying franchises would force you deeper into debt since you needed to pay off more of your loans. But it worked in a corollary way, the opposite of what you'd expect. The key to obtaining more financing was keeping the revenue flowing at the three Dunkin's we co-owned. Because we managed to jump-start the revenue, get it to high enough levels where we were making healthy profits annually, banks started knocking on our door to offer us capital, and we tended to stay with the banks that offered us money at the outset.

For most entrepreneurs, whether it's restaurant franchises, bicycle stores, florist shops, or garages, mastering the first business is the key to opening a second location. Perfecting that first business, which often can take a year or two, and sometimes three, you learn what works, who the best suppliers are, how to cut costs, how to hire staff, and how to appeal to customers.

And then you build up brand recognition, so people in your region know that the business is one to trust.

Moreover, we plowed our profits into an account that would enable us to open the second location and then the third. In that way, we didn't need another SBA loan or have to reach out for a bank loan, but instead used our windfall gains to keep expanding.

And we learned a considerable amount about the critical importance of locations. Where the franchise is situated is just as significant as what the food and coffee are like. And that holds true for many a business, whether it's an auto repair shop, a secondhand clothing store, or a hair salon.

We also figured out the importance of demographics. Now on the internet, you can tap different websites to ascertain the per capita income of any zip code, as well as the demographics of the audience—the ages and genders of the people who reside there—to see if that's a good fit for your business.

Attracting different audiences can also heighten your business. I call it "diversification." Rather than only appealing to middle-class clientele, I liked the idea of opening up businesses in affluent areas, working-class areas, and lower-class areas. Most people, no matter their income, like doughnuts, coffee, pizza, and smoothies, and appealing to different demographics and multiple audiences cushions the owner if times turn bad or if one neighborhood suffers a setback. I always considered Dunkin' recession proof because it prospered in tough times—and good times, too.

Dunkin' executives noticed our cash flow was spiking and started coming to us with opportunities for opening up new franchise locations in the Midwest. Banks lend to make money; loans are one of their key products. Minimizing risk is the name of their game, so they don't offer loans to most neophytes, only to those with proven track records, such as the one that we had built.

In fact, once you have proved yourself, banks encourage you to take out loans. You've already made them money by the interest you've paid, and the more capital borrowed, the greater their profits. We took out a loan and opened a fourth Dunkin' and kept expanding our weekly revenue. It was a win-win. The better the fast-food restaurants did profitwise, the more capital the banks offered us.

What I learned was a simple American truth about capitalism: The more money you make, the more capital you can raise, and the more your profits can accelerate. "Only the rich get richer" is a truism for a reason.

In the restaurant franchise world, like the financial universe and every other specialty, whom you know can go a long way to help you succeed. As I said earlier in the book, Harry Patel operated as a mentor to me. I viewed him as one of the kings of franchisees, because he owned over 80 Dunkin' Donuts and other franchises including Wingstop in the Midwest. He took a liking to me, knew from the Dunkin' execs that our stores were prospering, and asked me if I was interested in becoming his partner in several ventures. I seized the opportunity. Most of all, he told me, "You're hungry, and I like that."

Patel had something that made my life easier: a much longer track record of success in the restaurant franchise business. And that gave him easy access to credit and an ability to pay his mortgage payments without any difficulty. Even if there was a recession, Patel had the means to make those payments, and that made life easier for me, his partner.

Together we acquired three Dunkin's in the Quincy, Illinois, area, on the border near Missouri. Quincy was a town of about 50,000 people, and what attracted us was, at that point, there were no Dunkin's in the entire city. We opened a joint Dunkin' Donuts/Baskin-Robbins, and it was an instant hit, as if the denizens couldn't wait to try what they had been denied for years.

Patel was known as more of a financial guy, with deep pockets, and he left much of the operations to me, which was my forte. Those three stores were thriving, so we looked at St. Louis and acquired eight existing stores there. I was on my way to becoming a restaurant magnate.

What happened during the course of one day changed my restaurant franchisee life forever. I was driving around St. Louis with my real estate broker who lives there, looking for locations to build another Dunkin', and I wanted to eat lunch. I said to him, "I'm hungry, and I'm tired of scarfing down fast food."

I usually work out at the gym, and usually I'm so busy that I just choose what's closest to me and quickest, and that means consuming my own product: fast food. We passed by a Smoothie King, which I wasn't familiar with. "What's that?" I asked.

"Have you been living under a rock?" he retorted. "You never heard of Smoothie King? What's with that?"

"I'm from the Chicago area," I replied. "We have some Jamba Juices that I've stopped at, but I don't recall seeing any Smoothie Kings," I told him.

Once I tasted one of the smoothies that day, it was love at first sip. I avoided the drive-through, went inside, consumed the smoothie, saw the operations, and was impressed. When I returned home, I started doing my research. I saw that the average unit annual intake was rising, upward of $600,000, and I could see the potential for more.

Back in St. Louis, Harry and I were expanding our Dunkin's kingdom faster than you could say, "Doughnut and coffee, thank you." We had opened eight. But I was beginning to feel weighed down, because he was the financial guy, and I was the operating manager, running them all. Finally it felt like too much. He bought me out, and that gave me the capital to inaugurate some new Smoothie Kings.

I attended a Day of Discovery about opening a Smoothie King franchise and listened to Wan Kim, its CEO, who was of South Korean heritage, talk about opportunities with the franchise. We were both immigrants, and I felt a kinship with him. He seemed less corporate than other CEOs I had encountered, more authentic. He spoke more from the heart and didn't spout the usual scripted, political talk. He envisioned Smoothie King as the next great Starbucks kind of franchise that was primed to take off and proliferate. "Come join us," he urged the future franchisees, and I was ready, willing, and able to buy into the formula.

The point here is if you discover an idea that interests you, investigate it, as I did. It was the taste of Smoothie King's product that caught my attention, but I moved on to conduct my due diligence to see if it was a worthy business opportunity. And those details are true no matter what the business is.

I started with two Smoothie Kings in St. Louis, and they did well immediately. Then I signed up to acquire two more outlets and then five more. And by the end of 2019, right before the pandemic hit, I was up to owning 19 Smoothie Kings.

I felt that the trend in America was toward dining on low-calorie, healthier smoothies. And Smoothie King embodied this healthier lifestyle. Since I worked out at the fitness center and watched what I consumed, Smoothie King blended (no pun there) with my lifestyle.

And when the pandemic struck and attacked people faster who were obese and had a variety of physical ailments, the attraction to dine at Smoothie King intensified. People gravitated toward making healthier choices, and that enhanced our business model.

Hence, what I liked most about running a Smoothie King was that it represented something healthy that was good for you. Its mission was about ridding the diet of additives and sugar, and its drink was nourishing and salubrious.

To me, it was a once-in-a-lifetime opportunity. If I could catch this trend and it was on the upswing, I'd have myself a stable of profitable and fast-growing eateries. And with prices for acquiring outlets way down because of the pandemic, it was the right franchise at the right price, and in the fast-food business, timing is everything.

Smoothie Kings were easier to operate than Dunkin's. With Dunkin's, 70 percent of our business was morning, from 5 a.m. (depending on opening time) to 11 a.m., but at Smoothie King, sales stretched out for longer periods, namely at breakfast and lunch. Smoothies were considered meal replacements, and we didn't sell sandwiches there.

What I and my staff needed to master at Smoothie King was dealing with the blender and getting all the ingredients—for a fruit smoothie you'd need fruit, powder, and ice—just right. If there was too much liquid, it would be watery. Too much powder, and it didn't taste right. Not enough fruit, and it could be tasteless. But there were much fewer moving parts at Smoothie Kings, because you didn't have to make sandwiches, lattes, or espressos. If the employee knew how to handle the blender and ice machine well, the odds of doing a sterling job were very high.

While the speed of service is paramount at any fast-food eatery, it took a bit more time to get out our products at Smoothie King because the blender took some time to perform its magic. And most customers understood that fact and often weren't rushing the staffer to move faster. Still, we took speed of service seriously because no one wants to wait in a drive-through lane. Faster is always better than slower in the fast-casual restaurant world. So I'd test out the drive-throughs at Smoothie and taste the vanilla with peanut butter to make sure it tasted just right.

Peanut butter smoothies were often one of our best sellers (except with people with peanut allergies) and were one of my personal favorites. But when I tasted one, I was viewing it as an owner, not a consumer. I was gauging its consistency because I wanted it to taste the same no matter which one of our locations a guest stopped at. I wanted it to look the same, be poured into the cup a certain way, and be as delicious at one store as it was at the next.

We employed many of the same strategies that achieved success at Dunkin' at Smoothie King. We distributed coupons to take $2 off the price of a smoothie, and on our loyalty app, we offered "Free 20 ounces for your next visit." And those strategies boosted revenue so the Smoothie Kings that had been generating $500,000 annually were now producing $600,000 and $700,000.

What did it take to own two different brands of fast-food restaurant franchises simultaneously? I needed to build a strong foundation. And that meant making sure I created an overloaded system of hiring—choosing district managers with extra managers on board to step in in case of emergency to make sure every Smoothie King ran smoothly. I brought some managers over from Dunkin', paid them higher salaries, and put the team in place that I knew could run more than 20 Smoothie Kings and enable me to sleep soundly at night.

When the pandemic hit in early 2020, many of the older, more experienced franchisees of Smoothie King were looking to get out before Covid took over. Instead of the going rate for buying an existing franchise at $250,000 (now costing $350,000 or more), I was able to nab several of them for $135,000 each, a lowball figure that enabled me to proliferate my franchises in record-breaking time. As noted above, because of the strategies I learned at Dunkin', I was transforming each outlet's annual revenue from $500,000 to $700,000, so the cash flow was generating considerable profit.

Because the franchises were expanding faster than you could say "Smoothie to go" and we were on a growth path, I needed to start building up a staff with some infrastructure. The major ingredient in developing a staff was making sure you created a strong management team. Experienced managers knew how to navigate the highs and lows, during recessions and prosperous times, in tough times and downturns. I also wanted to ensure that my staff was trained well and therefore knew how to handle customer requests. I wanted the staff to be familiar with our products, understand them, be able to sell them, and do so in an upbeat and enthusiastic way. When I opened a new store, I would overhire—that is, recruit additional staff. Even though it added to payroll, I did it because I knew some staffers would jump ship and I didn't want to be burdened with insufficient staff. All of this came under the heading of "infrastructure," and it was critical to growth.

I called my umbrella company the "DLH Group" and in 2019 we had grown enough to move the back of the house operations from our house into a new office space. Luckily, I had already brought my wife into the business back in 2013 as an administrator. Later in 2020 to lighten the load, I hired a woman named Molly to answer calls, share payroll duties, handle the mail, and oversee organizing. Delegating to responsible staff makes life easy when you're operating over 40 restaurant franchises, or for that matter, other multiple businesses.

Once I had staffing in place, I could focus more on operations, or what I called "working in the field." I often say that my job as owner of fast-casual eateries entailed putting out fires or dealing with any disaster that strikes. Many of them were weather-related. You never know what is going to befall each outlet on any given day. A prime example—the flood in St. Louis in the summer of 2022.

On a July morning that summer, my phone started pinging. Weather alerts started cropping up on my phone about the possibility of a flood overtaking the city. I called my sister who lives in St. Louis and asked her for an assessment. Her area wasn't hit, but she said water was mounting up 6 inches with double that amount expected. In total, about 10 to 12 inches of rain pounded the city.

The manager of one Smoothie King contacted me in a panic. Water was rushing into the store. I urged her to make sure any leaks were patched up and then consider closing the store. When the water kept rising, I told the manager definitely to shut down the store and go home. Safety was the priority. Preserving human life was number one. We'd deal with the aftermath—and the insurance company—tomorrow. Several of our Smoothie Kings became inoperable because of power outages. So you close the stores and try to get the power company to turn the juice back on.

If an owner operates one store and it shuts down, all revenue stops. The glorious thing about being a multiple franchiser is that one store only generates one part of the revenue. So if the store closed down for several days, or even if a number of the St. Louis Smoothie Kings had to close, revenue would still pour in from the other outlets. Owning numerous restaurant brands stabilizes your cash flow.

The flood in St. Louis, despite its intensity, was short-lived. One store closed for a day, and another two days, and after that brief respite, normality returned. I didn't even file the insurance claims. One day's loss didn't warrant it. When the day was placid the next day, sales started booming. Everyone was so confined during the flood that coming outside for a smoothie for lunch hit the spot, and it compensated for the temporary closing.

Experience teaches an owner how to weather the storm. When I was starting out, had that flood occurred, I might have panicked. "What if the store is closed a week," I'd think to myself. I'd fear the worst. Now with over five years of experience and operating over 40 eateries, I'd take it all in stride and focus on figuring it out.

No matter what the brand is, Dunkin' or Smoothie King or Arby's, I've trained my district managers and managers to operate the Yonas way. Safety always comes first. Take care of yourself and your staff and your customers. Property can be replaced; people can't be. If there's smoke, call the fire department first and then call me. Problem-solve the situation. What can we do to fix the problem as quickly as possible? If you've been robbed, call the police department first and then notify me.

Stay calm. Don't panic. Panicking doesn't get you anywhere but flustered. Solve the problem. Assess the situation, and devise a solution. If streets are flooding, close the store and find a safe place. Don't be a hero. If you can't figure it out, call the experts tomorrow after everyone is safe and sound. That's the Yonas way.

I trained the teams to be empowered. If a customer is angry because he or she was served the wrong-flavor smoothie, don't call me. Make the customer happy. Prepare a new smoothie with the right flavor—problem solved.

To survive, you learn to adapt. It's the nature of owning multiple restaurants. Deliveries sometimes don't get there on time. Or employees are late. Or the blender or espresso machine breaks down. There is always something that can fall apart. But I've learned to manage my own stress level, go for long walks to clear my mind. Whatever happens today, tomorrow is another day, and another time to solve a problem.

When the oven falters, I don't think the sky is falling. I call the technician and get it fixed as quickly as possible. I've done it before, and I'll—we'll—do it again.

So now I owned two different brands, Dunkin' Donuts and Smoothie King, that were both thriving. Revenue was rising, and I had a handle on how to operate multiple brands. So why stop there?

I had gotten word that a large restaurant conglomerate Inspire Brands was about to acquire the Dunkin' brand, and it already owned Arby's, Sonic, and Jimmy John's. If it was strong enough to nab Dunkin', I figured opening an Arby's in my neck of the woods in the Chicago suburbs would be a winner as well.

In 2019, before the pandemic hit, a partner and I built an Arby's in Yorkville, Illinois, the area near where I live, which helped increase my stable of franchises. There was only one Arby's in that sector, and Arby's was rebranding itself with the

"We have the meats" national advertising campaign, which was taking off. So a partner and I built it.

For a long time, Arby's attracted a mostly working-class clientele. But then that marketing jingle of "We have the meats" helped lure a much wider audience including many Gen Xers and millennials. It was fast becoming a brand for all walks and ages of life.

I quickly learned that each restaurant franchise appealed to its own audience and found its niche at different times. So Dunkin' was mostly about breakfast with some lunch trade, but Arby's, which usually didn't open until 10 a.m. or 11 a.m., depending on whether they offer breakfast or not, attracted a lunch and dinner crowd.

Arby's was fast casual, and like the slogan suggested, guests came for roast beef, brisket, gyros, and fish sandwiches. It was meat-eaters who ruled, and the bulk of the customers were people who wanted a substantial meal. Salads clearly weren't the dominant menu item ordered.

Of course, we used coupons, often offering "two for one," to generate business and keep guests coming back.

And at Arby's, as in many other fast casuals, we tried to keep the line moving as quickly as possible. Arby's was a bit late to the mobile-app ordering game, but it quickly caught up.

And as my restaurant stable grew, I developed a team of managers who were seasoned and savvy. Some had been with me for four years, some three years, and they knew what worked and recognized how to handle staff. I sometimes felt that my Dunkin' Donuts locations ran themselves and needed minimal interference from me.

And then one day I went for lunch and found Chicken Salad Chick, a franchise that specialized in, as its name suggests, old-fashioned chicken salad. I was a bit surprised by the signature dish because I felt that chicken salad was bought at a supermarket or gas station, but here was a restaurant chain with that specialty. And when I dined there, I noticed, almost immediately, that 70 to 80 percent of the clientele were women

Why did that chain attract so many women and fewer men? Men tended to gravitate toward meatier items, which were heavy and more satisfying to them. I think because so many women made chicken salad at home, going out with their friends to dine on their dish was comforting to them. Since studies show that women do the majority of spending and choose which restaurant to go to, I knew that Chicken Salad Chick was going to be a prime addition to my franchising kingdom.

The chicken salad was made fresh daily, and the atmosphere was homespun. It was like dining in someone's kitchen. Compared to pizza, the salad was a relatively healthy meal, if you'll excuse the mayonnaise. In fact, the chicken was always steamed, not fried, making it nutritious.

That freshness stood out to me. With other franchises, it was frozen patties, but at Chicken Salad Chick, the chicken was made fresh every morning and was shredded in the morning, and that daily taste was a difference maker. The restaurant also had other salads as fresh as the chicken salad. And so I added one more franchise to the group.

The majority of our business at Chicken Salad Chick was at lunch, but the restaurant also generated a healthy segment of catering. Businesses ordered lunch for their employees or for business meetings, and who doesn't like chicken salad?

It also tended to attract a very loyal audience, who would dine there twice a week and never get tired of ordering chicken salad, though there was an array of sandwiches and salads on the menu.

One of my business partners owned a Rosati's Pizza in the Chicago area, selling deep-dish pizza that the Second City was known for. Since my stable of eateries now contained doughnuts, smoothies, roast beef sandwiches, and chicken salads, I was looking to expand my reach. Pizza seemed a natural fit.

In doing my homework, I saw that some outlets of Rosati's Pizza generated a whopping $3 million in sales. That number impressed me, and my partners and I wanted to get aboard that train. And many of the Rosati's Pizzas had a separate pub station, and that meant beer and liquor sales, which were high margin.

My goal in acquiring the Rosati's Pizza in Plainfield, Illinois, was to diversify. Everyone knows that people will flock to a McDonald's for a burger one night, and then the next night want to dine on something different, like tacos or pizza. So adding a pizza shop to the doughnuts, smoothies, and roast beef eateries meant attracting new customers for a different meal.

It also meant that if smoothie sales trended downward, and doughnut revenue leveled off, my businesses could still sail by on pizza sales. Rosati's offered me a new market to tap, which could stabilize sales. In fact, we acquired a second Rosati's Pizza in Largo, Florida, a suburb of Tampa. The one that we opened in 2023 attracted a bevy of snowbirds in the winter from Canada, Chicago, and New York and New Jersey who were keen on avoiding cold and snow.

Even when you consider fluctuating revenue on a seasonal basis, owning a pizza establishment made sense. For a variety of reasons, smoothie sales dipped in the winter when many guests preferred warmer food. But pizza sales surged in winter when it was cold in the Midwest and people opted to consume food that comforted them in snowy, icy climates. So having these five brands meant income would be steadier without facing the traditional winter blues.

Diversifying brands offered our business a host of benefits. For one thing, we were marketing to different tastes and demographics and reached a broader audience. And as said before, if sales dropped at one location, invariably they rose at another, so our net revenue stayed steady. It cushioned us against any kind of downturn or weather catastrophe in a certain area.

That also meant that because I was based in Illinois, I was managing a team that was 1,000 miles away. But nowadays there are a litany of tools at your fingertips that enable you to manage from afar, including cameras in the store and metrics that let you know how each store is doing in its sales per items and at different times of the day. We use WhatsApp to stay in touch with managers on a daily basis, enabling us to connect in real time. Technology enables you to manage long distance in many more ways than was true 30 years ago.

But I wasn't finished yet. One of my Smoothie King partners, Faisal Raja, told me about two women in Las Vegas who had launched a bakery, first out of their kitchen and then as a retail shop, Nothing Bundt Cakes. Dena Tripp and Debbie Shwetz launched the bakery in 1997, and there are now over 430 bakery locations in 40 states and Canada!

When I told my wife about the bakery, she lit up and said, "I love bundt cake. We don't eat sweets very much so it would be a perfect treat." She sold me on the idea.

You know the expression "It's the icing on the cake"? That's where Nothing Bundt Cakes stood out. They are a sweet confection with a hole in the middle. Those lemon raspberry bundt cakes, miniature bundtlets, and decorated bundt cakes oozed icing and won over just about anyone with a sweet tooth. People knew bundt cakes, they trusted them, and Nothing Bundt Cakes had tremendous name recognition in many regions.

The cakes were a crowd-pleaser for families throughout the country. At times of stress and recession and political upheavals, bundt cakes are something to fall back on. They're sugary sweet

and satisfying and give you what I always consider instant gratification. When you need a reward and a pick-me-up, bundt cakes
hit the spot.

As with Chicken Salad Chick, the target audience was
women. We bought two Nothing Bundt Cakes franchises, and
they prospered immediately, though we eventually sold one. Not
only did we sell sweets, but we sold party items, decor, and gifts
and did a considerable amount of catering of birthday parties
and anniversaries. Products could be ordered online and picked
up at the stores, and they provided another revenue stream to
add some additional income.

Now I was overseeing six brands at once. So the key for me
was mastering multitasking. How many activities could I do at
once? How could I keep track of the Dunkin' Donuts, Smoothie
King, Arby's, Rosati's Pizza, Chicken Salad Chick, and now
Nothing Bundt Cakes and make sure everything was operating at
full speed at all locations?

Having a great staff is primary. Understanding restaurant
operations is also critical. As is keeping track of one major ingredient: the margins. If my margins were strong enough, profit
would flow, mortgage payments would be made, salaries would
be covered, and everything would be running on all cylinders. I
had systems in place at each eatery, depending on the brand, to
ensure a smooth-flowing operation.

I learned to empower my staff more and more. I couldn't be
at 47 eateries at once. I needed the multi-unit manager to oversee the general manager, guide the store managers, and lead the
assistant managers.

Key Tips

FOR WHAT WORKS BEST WHEN YOU'RE EXPANDING YOUR BUSINESS

TIP #1
Diversify Your Business

Rather than owning just Dunkin' franchises, I opted to add a smoothie shop, roast beef restaurant, pizza shop, chicken salad eatery, and bundt cake bakery to my portfolio. The more brands I had, the more diversified my businesses were. Spreading things out meant that if smoothie sales declined, pizza sales might rise, and everything would be stable, and profits would continue at the same pace. It cushioned me during downturns to own so many different types of food franchises. The more revenue streams I had going at once, the better off I was. And that would be true for any entrepreneur, whether he or she owned a bicycle shop, an auto repair shop, or even an app.

TIP #2
Find Like-Minded Partners

In several of these businesses, I minimized my risk and capital expenditure by finding like-minded restaurant franchisees and entrepreneurs who were on my wavelength and were willing to invest. That meant I needed fewer loans, and minimizing the number of loans meant I could expand my stable faster.

TIP #3
Master Problem-Solving

You can guarantee when you own a restaurant that something will always break down. The espresso machine. The blender. The drive-through telecom. Repairing it and not getting distracted with worry are the ways to get the job done and problem-solve.

TIP #4
Empower Your Staff

I can't be at 47 eateries at once. Impossible. So I had to train my staff to do things the Yonas way, and that would lead to getting the job done.

TIP #5
Find a Partner Who Has Access to Capital

I wasn't looking for a well-heeled partner, but when I got to know Harry Patel and we formed a connection, it helped vault me to a higher level. He was well connected, owned over 80 franchises, and had access to capital, and partnering with him led me to co-owning multiple franchises. Our relationship did take its natural course and concluded, but it was his expertise and track record that put me on a path to success. Could I have done this without him? Likely I could have, but it would have taken several years to play out. He put me on the express track to success.

TIP #6
Focus on the Managers

When you own seven, or eight, or ten, or a dozen restaurant franchises, you can't be at all locations at once. Even with video cameras, you're observing things from afar. It's the individual managers that steer the ship, like a captain on a boat. Yes, you need to please your customers. But without the skilled manager helming the restaurant, you'll never meet their needs. Hence, I spent the bulk of my energy on hiring the right managers with the requisite experience and training them in Dunkin's or Smoothie King's methods, and most of all, in the Yonas way.

To me, you're only as good as the people you have, particularly your managers. They are the engine that drives the business. They understand the business and know how to collaborate with employees and relate to customers.

TIP #7
When You're Making Money, Use It to Grow the Business

The thing about capitalism is, once you start making money, you can tap into it to expand your business, open more outlets, buy more stores. Making money makes it easier to become more profitable. And once you've taken out a loan and repaid it in a timely fashion, you're likely to be offered more loans. And that means growing your business, which in my case meant going from owning 3 Dunkin' Donuts to owning over 10 Smoothie Kings.

TIP #8
It's All About the Cash Flow

Ultimately, what enabled me to succeed was increasing the bottom-line profit of each franchise. We kept our costs down, monitored food ordering, used devices such as coupons to boost business, and kept generating more revenue at each location. Our profit increased, we could pay the mortgage fees with ease, and then we could keep expanding. Making more money helped us make more money. We fixed the bottom line and kept generating success.

TIP #9
Owning Multiple Businesses Can Solve Several Problems

The more franchises you own, and the more cash flow you can generate, the better off you are. If you own 47 stores and smoothies go out of season in winter, the brisket sandwiches at Arby's hit the spot and keep the register clanking away.

TIP #10
Avoid Brand Conflicts

Owners of Dunkin' Donuts are not permitted to acquire competitors, so Starbucks will never be in my portfolio. However, I could operate a Popeye's, which isn't a competitor.

TIP #11
Operations Transcend the Specialty

Restaurants are places where people dine, and it really doesn't matter if you're serving up smoothies, doughnuts, or egg sandwiches. Operations are operations. And you're always dealing with customers, and the emphasis is on treating them right and getting the order out quickly and accurately, whether it's a pineapple smoothie, a chicken salad sandwich, or a bundt cake. Greet the customers, welcome them, get to know them, treat them right, and create an atmosphere where they'll want to return—no matter what the restaurant brand.

TIP #12
Keep the Margins High

Watching your food costs and keeping them under control, making sure you order the right inventory, and maintaining your portion controls are all key ingredients to shoring up your margins, whether it's pizza or roast beef.

TIP #13
Minimize Food Waste

Keeping food waste to a minimum heightens your margins. For example, I had a Dunkin's employee whom I saw discard about two dozen doughnuts, which weren't bought by the end of the day, in the trash can. When I saw him do that, I took out a $20 bill and tossed it into the wastepaper basket under his watchful eye. "What are you doing?" he asked me, consternated and startled. I wasn't trying to disrespect him, and he and I had a trusting relationship.

In fact, I saw this as a "teachable moment" to let him know that food waste is taken seriously and cuts into our margins.

"I'm doing what you're doing," I replied. "Tossing money out the window," I added. I once did research about how much food was wasted in the various Dunkin' stores and learned that each Dunkin's outlet threw out about $50,000 a year of merchandise. If we could reduce that by half, I'd save $25,000—and my profits would rise by that amount. Now we print out how many doughnuts we sell, say, on August 9, 2022, so we can prepare the right amount a year from that day, taking into account that weather can affect sales. Training employees to reduce waste is just one example of how to keep margins high.

The more I could forecast what I would sell each day, based on the past year's performance, the more I could reduce waste, help the environment, and boost my margins and profit. We studied charts to know how many doughnuts we sold on August 9 and how many smoothies we sold on September 1, and ordered food and prepared it based on past performance. We weren't always right, but reducing waste meant expanding profits.

CHAPTER 8

IT STARTS WITH YOUR OWN SELF-PERCEPTION

Why Being an Immigrant Is an Advantage, Not a Detriment

E veryone in America defines success differently; there's not just one way of looking at it. For an immigrant like me, my outlook emanates from my growing up in Africa. Having a roof over your head on that continent was a sign of making it. But coming to America meant a raft of opportunities, involving getting educated and being able to make something of yourself.

Once I started to open my franchises and multiply them, and was making good money, I felt successful. I bought a larger house, bought a car, and had all the accoutrements of success.

But making it breeds pressure. Sometimes when people see you do well, it creates pressure on you. They get envious of you, and want things from you, and have a tendency to belittle you behind your back. "Why is he making it, and I'm not?" "What makes him think so much of himself?"

Sometimes I purposely hide how well I do. I don't wear an expensive watch because I don't want people to judge me. And I'll admit that some days, being successful triggers some anxiety of having to sustain it while dealing with other people's reactions. But most times, I just feel humble and grateful.

And I've learned the methods that work best for me to relieve my stress and establish balance in my life. I play golf, or ride a bicycle, or go on long walks, and it's almost always physical activity and exertion that relax my mind and body. That's what works best for me. But success can be a double-edged sword.

The trap is letting yourself get too comfortable and yielding to too many materialistic desires. Not allowing yourself to get complacent entails avoiding getting stuck in the desire to own too many material things. Or as I call it, "owning too much stuff." If all you dream about is possessing the trendiest leather coat for $5,000, or state-of-the-art headphones, then there's a problem.

Whenever I see myself slipping into self-satisfaction, I slow myself down. Or do something to make myself feel uncom-fortable. When I opened my first Dunkin' Donuts franchise, it was time to take a step back and celebrate. Did I buy myself a Lamborghini or Rolex watch? I didn't. My wife, Kristie, and I dined at an upscale restaurant and toasted ourselves, but it was a rather modest celebration. There was too much to do, and too many things could go wrong. I needed to keep myself on my toes so I could respond to any emergency downtown or any setback (or all of the above). I needed to have funds in reserve to shelter me from any potential storm.

Some people starting out can easily get depressed and deflated, feel stuck, and think that they're making minimal progress. But here's the question I ask to differentiate the future winners from those who stumble and falter. How passionate are you about your entrepreneurial idea, about your game plan, and about your hopes? Are you doing it mostly for the money, or do you love the idea of becoming an entrepreneur?

If you're only motivated by dollar signs, there will be a problem. You need to love what you do, be motivated by it, and be driven by it. Not just the money.

When I was starting out and people asked what my future plans were, my refrain was "I want to be my own boss." At the time, I wasn't certain exactly what route I would take to get there, but I was enthused and energized by the idea of entrepreneurship of some kind.

When I left the US Army, I spoke with a career counselor, and she asked about my plans. I replied that I wanted to be my own boss but wasn't sure of the specifics—yet. She was reassuring. "You'll find a way if you're passionate about it," she said. And she was right. I took some detours along the way, but I finally arrived at owning multiple restaurant franchises and never looked back.

I've met many people starting out who talk themselves into depression, dejection, and failure, without giving themselves a sufficient chance at succeeding. You need to start your plan early on. For example, start thinking about friends and family that you can tap for investing in your initial project. These are the people who believe in you, who know and trust you, and the hope is that some of them have some money to invest.

Write down a simple business plan of what you want to do, and who you think are the best candidates to inject capital. Starting out, you'll have a tougher time with the big banks, so think locally. Is there a local credit union you belong to? A local savings bank where you or your parents know the manager? A local nonprofit that has an investing arm? Think creatively.

Maybe opening a restaurant is too costly. So start with a food truck. How much would it cost to buy a truck? Lease it? What specialty can trigger a positive customer response? What void is there to fill? Is there a farmer's market in your area or neighborhood that permits food trucks? Whom do you know who owns one? Whom can you tap to ask questions about starting out? Be realistic, but once you start with a game plan, start taking steps to make it happen.

And it doesn't have to be food-related. The internet is often the least expensive way to start a business. You don't need real estate, you don't need to hire contractors and construction crews, and you often can launch a business with minimal capital. I'd advise tracking down people who have started businesses via apps and see how they've done it. Or check YouTube and watch and listen and take notes on successful entrepreneurs. I heard about someone who, with very modest funds, started a used tire website and prospered. Hence, find a niche that no one has explored and run with it.

When I was starting out and had minimal savings, I kept hearing the saying, "Save for a rainy day." But I've shifted my lens to think of it as "Save so you don't have a rainy day." The point is to put enough money aside so that if your car breaks down, you have enough savings to fix it, or if your roof runs a leak, you can repair it. Whatever life throws at you, once you've put aside enough money to prepare for it, you feel liberated and relieved. When I was starting out, if one Dunkin' Donuts faced a setback, it could disrupt my cash flow and damage the business. So savings were necessary to withstand any obstacles.

If you're starting out and have dreams, get yourself into a mindset to learn as much as you can to achieve your dreams. Talk to people. If your goal is to open a modest Subway franchise in an adjacent neighborhood, start working at it. Pepper the owner of the Subway in your neighborhood with questions. Ask questions such as "How did you start out?" "How did you capitalize the business?" "How did you raise money? Did you ask friends and family for money?" "Was taking out a loan necessary? If so, what was done to secure it?" "Did you have to hire an attorney? How did you find one?"

Start developing your business plan as early as possible. It doesn't have to be a 100-page document, but could be a 10-page one. What's the goal of the business? Why is it needed? Where will it be? What void is being filled? Why does this neighborhood need this business at this time? Whom will it appeal to? How much capital must be raised? Why are you the one to launch it?

I encourage my managers to train their best employees to replace them if they are promoted or move on to another job. And if they're afraid to guide their employees because they fear it could lead to their losing their job or being replaced by them, they don't last long in my organization. They have to be willing to lead and therefore train their successor, and that's how organizations replenish and move on.

Too many people in their twenties, for a variety of reasons, haven't mastered the basics. Showing up on time or early is the best way to impress your manager and boss. Spending too much time listening to podcasts or Spotify or sending TikTok images to your friend while on the job is unacceptable and distracts the employees from doing their job, and doing it well.

Nowadays I see too many Gen Zs who want to become YouTube millionaires. It's like years ago, the best basketball players in my Chicago suburban neighborhood dreamed of becoming a professional NBA player. What they didn't realize is, that's equivalent to winning the lottery. One out of a hundred thousand college basketball stars sustains a career in the NBA. For most, it's a pipe dream, not realistic for most people, beyond the likes of Steph Curry and LeBron James and about 400 others. Even if you take into account the professional basketball minor leagues, there will likely be only a thousand jobs, and that's it.

When you're starting out working at a restaurant, observe as much as you can. Within the restaurant franchise, see how the manager orders food and which vendors are used. Specifically, which vendors are used for meats? Vegetables? Napkins? How much time in the schedule does the manager devote to ordering. Learn the ins and outs. How are orders tracked? What software is used? How does the manager ensure delivery in time?

How does the manager deal with employees, which, as I've said, is critical. How does the manager defuse conflicts with customers? Turn a negative gripe into a positive situation? Handle the multicultural kitchen staff who often come from Mexico, China, Ecuador, or Ghana? How does he or she juggle so many activities at once and still stay on top of everything?

As I've said, learn as much as you can. If you are an immigrant, the more you become Americanized and understand the culture, the easier it will be to succeed. And take pride in your original heritage. I love when people ask me, "What do Ethiopians like to eat?" And "Where's the best Ethiopian restaurant in Chicago? Are there any in the suburbs?"

Early on, I became a sports fan. "How are your Cubbies doing?" I'd ask some of the customers at McDonald's? Or "How are your White Sox doing?" I'd ask other customers, many of whom despised the Cubbies. The more acclimated I became to American culture, the more I fit in.

I encourage my staff members, where appropriate, to attend junior college, as I did. I attended the College of DuPage in a Chicago suburb, and it taught me many things. It wasn't very expensive, and I could improve my vocabulary and speech, and many of the professors were totally engaged with their students. You're not there to party because most students live locally, commute from home, and are studying to forge a career and enhance their learning.

Several of my professors were encouraging to me, and yet I acknowledged early on that the academic life of pursuing degrees wasn't for me. Moving from an associate's degree to a bachelor's degree can put students into debt for $40,000 (about the average) or more, and I wasn't interested in saddling myself with that much. If, after they graduate, they get a job earning $50,000, they'll spend years paying off their debt and see the interest rate escalate. That wasn't for me.

One professor said you can thrive without earning an associate's degree. Plenty of people prosper without an academic degree. Yet when I told my parents that I was dropping out without earning a degree, they were crushed. They figured that education was the only way to thrive, and they were devastated. But higher learning isn't for everyone, and as I said, it wasn't for me, despite the fact that I urge my employees to take advantage of inexpensive, local junior colleges.

I instill those goals in my staff. If you work 8 hours a day in the United States—or even more, say, 10 or 12 hours—you can get ahead, save money, and make your mark. Whether you are an immigrant, are from the working class, are poor, or are from a tough neighborhood, if you know how to save, and not just spend, spend, spend, you can put money away and make some dreams come true.

Once you make it, you have to be aware of the trap: complacency. That's when you get overly satisfied, take things for granted, sit back, and rest on your laurels. That's like falling into the ocean and drowning. It can undermine or vex the best of us—

immigrants or not—and I try hard not to succumb to it. With the restaurant franchises, the buck stops with me, so that helps me avoid giving in to feeling too satisfied. Even when I'm on vacation, I get calls from district managers to handle a crisis, so that helps me avoid the dreaded complacency.

Still, immigrants, especially, need to take a step back and also feel satisfied about their lives here. Even those who are poor or working class can have running water, showers in the morning, and air-conditioning. In third-world countries those are considered luxuries. Here they're a starting point to catapult you into success.

When I was coming up in the ranks of restaurant franchises, I encountered several role models. Many immigrants, particularly people from India, started to become multiple restaurant franchisees. "If they could do it," I thought, "so could I." And I did. Seeing and meeting them at those national rollout franchise meetings was very inspiring.

My immigrant background also fine-tuned my hiring and recruiting practices. When I was working, I was eager to learn, ready to do just about anything to get the job done, and possessed high energy. While I was open to hiring different personalities, when I owned my first Dunkin' and then after we expanded, I recruited dynamic staff members who were motivated to learn. I could teach someone the skills to make a good cup of espresso, but having the right attitude was a more innate outlook.

I had some problems with some employees who felt entitled, particularly those who were in their twenties. People in that age group seem to think that the world owes them something and that going out of their way, beyond the scope of duty, is beyond them. Because of my immigrant background that triggers some issues for me, I need to devise ways to reach them to instill in them a whole new outlook.

Many of the immigrants I've hired operate the way I did. They're hungry to learn and to move up, and that often leads to becoming top performers. Sometimes they need help with writing skills or communication skills, but that can be adjusted on the job.

And many of them possessed certain traits in common. They were frugal, kept building their savings, didn't overspend, and were economically savvy. Living with less became a way of life, as did building equity for the future. I understood their frugal ways: Saving meant more to me than spending on gadgets.

What I ended up doing was mixing immigrant ways with American know-how. That combination, grinding it out day after day to work at fast-food restaurants and then own a painting-and-cleaning business, a fitness center, and finally one restaurant franchise contributed to my success. I took the hard work of being an immigrant and parlayed it into the American way of saving to build wealth.

I sacrificed my weekends for years, but that was part of my success formula. Off days? They were few and far between. I had to keep digging in, extending myself, developing the business, attracting new customers, moving from one venture to the next. I kept thinking, "If I can work this hard in my twenties and thirties, and save and save, then by the time I turn 45, I will have it all figured out and have saved enough money to do what I want when I want to do it. I can retire and live off passive income, and my children will be off to college."

Looking into the future, and after having recently turned 40 years old, I decided one of my goals would be to create passive income. Now that doesn't mean retiring, but it does entail finding ways to work fewer hours and still generate regular income. A January 27, 2023, *New York Times* article suggested that some ways to create passive income are to "sell courses, e-books or

other products online; offer property on short-term rental plat-
forms like Airbnb and Vrbo; or even buy and maintain vend-
ing machines." I've even looked into buying a storage facility
to boost passive income. Or maybe sell some franchises and see
what income the land, which we own, can bring us.

One of the ways that I plan on being set up for the future
at age 45 is investing in real estate. Buying properties is critical to my long-term plan, and properties require considerably
less hands-on managing than a restaurant franchise. And you can
always hire a property manager to oversee things.

SOME THOUGHTS ABOUT BEING
AN IMMIGRANT-BUSINESSPERSON

I end this chapter with a focus on being an immigrant and a
businessperson, but everyone who has ever faced prejudice will
appreciate what I went through and learned—and just about all
of us can empathize even if we haven't gone through it ourselves.

I had to overcome prejudice and preconceived notions when
many of my peer franchise owners learned that I was Ethiopian.
I remember one of my first quarterly Dunkin' meetings for all
operators in Chicago when we acquired our first franchise.
There were about a couple of hundred people at the meeting,
and the officials running things announced the names of the new
franchisees. When they said, "Yonas Hagos," I waved my hands
in recognition. Afterward, some of my fellow operators came up
to me.

"You're not Indian, are you? I thought you'd be Indian with the
name 'Yonas Hagos,'" one franchisee said. He was of Indian heritage, and as stated earlier, there were numerous Indian franchisees.

At the hotel bar after the conference, I encountered similar assumptions. "Did you play for the Chicago Bears?" one franchisee inquired.

"Did your parents get rich and provide the money to start the business?" another asked.

To this question I replied, "No, I used my brains."

I became numb to their prejudicial comments. Rather than just accepting me for who I was, a hardworking immigrant who started at the bottom and strove to succeed, people injected their own assumptions. Some of the people were wealthy, and some weren't. That didn't seem to matter. I just learned early that you needed a thick skin to prosper in the United States. And by thick skin, I mean not taking things personally, not taking their comments to heart, not getting dejected by their lack of comprehending that an immigrant like me could succeed. And that thick skin served me well dealing with customers, employees, and just about everybody in life.

Not being affected by other people's prejudices and slights is a very liberating feeling. It allows you to control the situation, rather than get undermined by someone else's ignorance. If you sit there and sulk, it affects your performance, throws you off your A game, and weakens your ability to do the best job you can. I also learned when I was in the military that staying confident in all situations almost guarantees success. Not getting flustered, not showing weakness, not being indecisive, but knowing who you are enables you to stay in control of situations.

And I also adapted my own behavior. When I was attending those Dunkin' franchise meetings, I purposely changed my speech. I'd employ a more literate vocabulary to show that I was educated, and I'd dress casually in jeans and a polo shirt. I wanted to demonstrate that I was educated and had the know-how to operate a Dunkin' franchise. I wasn't just a guy from the hood.

I'm also religious. I put my faith in God, and when I've encountered racist people who make nasty, demeaning comments, I tell myself that the world is filled with many more good people than nasty ones. America is the most generous country on earth, and so many Americans treat charity as a national value. When people tell me, "Go back to your country," which I've heard more times than I can count, I've said to them, "Other than Native Americans who were here first, we're all immigrants. I'm no different than you and your forebears."

Key Tips

FOR HOW IMMIGRANTS CAN GET AHEAD

TIP #1
Maintain That Immigrant's Edge

Immigrants know how to work hard. We arrive on time, stay late, don't mind getting our fingernails dirty, and want to learn as much as possible. We want to absorb as much as possible and learn many things, and, yes, we want to move up. But sustaining that immigrant's edge is one of the first steps toward achieving your dreams.

TIP #2
Consider Starting Out Small

Maybe opening a restaurant can cost a quarter of million dollars with construction costs and permits, so think about leasing a food truck, for example. Make your name that way.

TIP #3
Think Angels and Friends

Most people tap their family and friends for capital to launch a business. They know you, like you, know your skills and tenacity. Start making a list of people you can tap. Begin your business plan to show them. Do your homework. Consult your accountant on the financials.

TIP #4
Ask Targeted Questions

Both the owner of the restaurant and the manager are founts of knowledge. Pepper them with questions about how they started. Anoint them as role models. Most people are eager to help.

TIP #5
Observe as Much as You Can

How does a restaurant manager juggle his or her time? Take notes. How much time is spent for restaurant inventory? How much time is spent with the kitchen staff? How does the manager prepare the maître d' to greet guests? What happens when the grill breaks down?

TIP #6
Become Americanized

Learn as much about the American culture as you can. The more cultural references you master, the more you'll fit in, whether it's TV, movies, sports, or podcasts.

TIP #7
Start Developing a Business Plan

It's too easy to get hard on yourself when you're starting out. You're only a busboy or a dishwasher and think you're stuck. But you're not. You're only starting out. These jobs are springboards to propel you into action if you plan ahead. Start thinking now about your business plan—what it entails and how you'll be raising money.

TIP #8
View Being an Immigrant as a Positive

Too many immigrants see themselves as being at a deficit compared with native-born people. And there are language and cultural issues to overcome. But like I did, coming to the United States knowing two words, once you master the language, you can start making your plans for success. Being an immigrant means you know what hard work is, you know how to go the extra mile, and you're not reluctant to work more than eight hours a day to get the job done to surge ahead in your career. Once you see being an immigrant in a more positive light, you are ripe to ascend and move yourself up any career ladder. Yes, the point is changing one's self-image of being an immigrant. Once it's perceived as positive, it's easy to move up and get ahead and not be held back.

TIP #9
Start Saving Early

One of the prime movers for getting ahead in the United States is amassing savings and capital. Avoiding overspending and getting too much in debt is critical to an immigrant's (and this applies to poor and working-class people, too) ability to forge ahead. It's too easy to spend, often on "stuff" that you don't need. Start a saving plans. Call a financial planner. Put aside 10 or 15 percent of what you earn. That'll give you leverage to get ahead—as it did for me.

TIP #10
Avoid Complacency

Once you have a steady job and start saving money, don't sit back and think you have it made. Complacency has done in many an immigrant. Now you're ready to start moving up and investing your savings or getting involved in some endeavor that moves you up on the corporate chart or in your entrepreneurial endeavors.

TIP #11
Use Your Immigrant Instincts

Hiring the right people has been critical to my success as a franchise owner. I can sense when future employees are hungry, want to move up, and are energized by the possibility. Why? That was myself starting out at McDonald's and Burger King and using those entry-level jobs as a springboard to move up and on. Being an immigrant enables you to tap future success. Trust your instincts.

TIP #12
Develop Your Thick Skin to People's Prejudices

I've been slighted, belittled, overlooked, and put down by customers and fellow owners. That's their problem. When someone asks if I played for the Chicago Bears football team and that's how I came to own a Smoothie King, I laugh and move on. Don't let people's assumptions undermine you. Once you don't take their comments personally, and can respond in a jocular way, it frees you to move on and keep going to achieve your goals.

CHAPTER **9**

ENOUGH WITH THE FRANCHISES

Here's What It Takes to Innovate, Follow Your Dreams, and Open Up Independent Businesses

You know by now that I've been working in fast-food restaurant franchises from the time I was 14, and since I recently turned 40, that was over 25 years ago. Over the last dozen years, I've operated 47 restaurant franchises with a varied portfolio of Dunkin', Smoothie King, Arby's, Chicken Salad Chick, Nothing Bundt Cakes, and others. I decided it was time for me to branch off on my own, use the knowledge I've garnered about how to run a franchise eatery, and develop my own signature eatery. It was Yonas's time, a period for me to flex my muscles and explore my own passions, rather than follow the lead of others.

And what makes franchises so successful, their consistency, is exactly what I needed a break from. The fact that you could walk into a Dunkin' on Michigan Avenue in Chicago, or one near Times Square in New York City, or one on Constitution Avenue in Washington, DC, and the coffee would taste the same, and so would the sugary doughnuts, and so would the breakfast sandwiches—and a good thing that they did since this was Dunkin's selling point. But I needed to break through that uniformity and forge my own path.

Everything in the franchise business is about duplicating, not originating. What I yearned to do was not to replicate, but to develop original restaurants with a distinctive theme and menu.

Since I travel extensively across the United States to visit many of my eateries, I've turned into a foodie. I like tasty, original food, and that drew me to starting Silver Fox Bar & Grill in my hometown of Yorkville, Illinois.

What I wanted to do in Yorkville was build a swanky, tasteful, elegant but neighborhood bar and tavern like one you might find in Las Vegas. My hometown may be small, but it's growing and deserves an independent eatery that could fit in on the Las Vegas strip. With all my 25 years of experience in the restaurant industry, I knew that I could create a special place in the southwestern suburbs of Chicago.

The first thing I did to launch my dream was to identify the right partners. Since I wanted to start a business where food, a bar, and drinks would play a pivotal role, I joined with Brandon Partridge, an experienced restaurateur in this area, and Joe Porretta, a seasoned chef. Our goal was to develop a swanky restaurant that still had a down-home feel, one where you could dine on a $16 burger with fries or have a high-end steak for over $50 a person. We wanted to establish an upscale neighborhood bar and grill that had something for everyone, where you could dine in an upscale way or choose not to break the bank.

What made revamping this restaurant and turning it into a new concept special was that my partners and I could finance it without obtaining a loan. In fact, we bought the real estate on which the restaurant was located. That took all the financial pressure off. When you don't have debt, you're running an eatery anxiety-free. OK, maybe not totally without anxiety, but owning the land lessened the stress. Owning the real estate and the building lifted enormous financial pressure off my back.

Looking into the past, I remember taking out that first loan to open my first franchise, Anytime Fitness Center. Now that was stressful. Without the help of a loan from the fitness company, I'm not sure how I would ever have scraped up enough capital to open. Every national bank, local bank, and credit union rejected me, saying I was too risky—too young and too unproven.

Now onto originality. In 2020, we acquired a long-established eatery called Blackstone, which was known as a high-end steakhouse and continental dining spot. It was on a well-traveled state road, so everyone in the area knew it. Hence, when we took it over, it was a recognized destination, even though we soon changed the name, the decor, the menu, and the ambiance. I oversaw the entire remodeling and turned it into the classy bistro that I had dreamed about opening.

We also retained much of Blackstone's staff because they knew Yorkville, knew what the clientele were seeking, and could make the transition to a new menu and atmosphere. When the customers walked in, the music was hip and soothing, kind of like a Las Vegas eatery. And we had a large deck and patio area so, weather permitting, the restaurant could function as a four-season outdoor and indoor eatery. My goal was to make it a fun place, where memories could be made, for dining out, special occasions, and catered affairs.

We had a variety of different menus including buffet-style brunches, Sunday brunches, fancy pasta dishes for dinner, shell tower clams, a special grouper, six types of burgers—you name it. And then there were the cocktails, including a pumpkin spice martini that had a kick to it.

When we launched Silver Fox Bar & Grill, we decided on the menu, the atmosphere, and the culture, and then we executed the marketing. If we observed a clever idea at another establishment, we could introduce it and bring it to life without having to gain approval. It was our baby, our restaurant, and we determined its existence, set its themes, and made any adaptations where necessary. No one was watching over us, telling us what to do.

And we were saving the almost 11 percent fees you pay the franchiser on your monthly revenue. That boils down to about 5.9 percent in royalty fees and 5 percent in marketing. So if we were a franchise and generated $750,000 in revenue for the month, about $80,000 would be sent to the franchiser. When you own your own business, there are no royalty fees, and you conduct your own marketing. It felt very freeing.

At Silver Fox Bar & Grill, we decided what to do. No parent company had to authorize what we did, or reject it, or comment on it. We were free as a bird in the sky to do what we wanted. If I needed to acquire a pizza oven, I did and didn't have to submit a request form. We could take control, seize the opportunity, and buy it.

Our target market was predominantly an upper-middle-class, white-collar clientele that befits the suburb of Yorkville, where the average income was $103,000. But it was also the kind of local tavern where you could dine for under $25 a person if you were so inclined. Most people dressed up; men wore sport jackets and tailored slacks rather than a T-shirt and blue jeans or cutoffs.

Moreover, though Yorkville was considered a modest-sized town, its population was increasing. For years, it was a stable town of 20,000 people. But when crime rose in nearby Chicago, many urban folks headed for the suburbs, and Yorkville became a top alternative. The town population had grown to more than 25,000 people, and expanding a town's population by 25 percent is quite a boost. I saw the opportunity to shake up the town, fill a void, appeal to two different audiences, and put my own stamp on both of them. Yorkville was growing in stature and influence and affluence, and the restaurant industry hadn't developed with it. We wanted to create something that wasn't there before: upscale and classy, theatrical and slightly over the top. In a sense, we wanted to put on a show through the restaurant's decor plus menu.

Having the two partners also made life easier, and even though I was the restaurant operator in chief, both partners possessed their own niches. Joe Porretta, an expert chef, was responsible for concocting new recipes and keeping tuned in to changing client tastes. Brandon Partridge served as key liaison with our manager and as overall operator and maintained control of our inventory. And I oversaw the big picture. I concentrated on the development and construction of new restaurants. Our friendship deepened as we continued to run it, and that is a rare and high compliment for three partners to get along so well.

We had photos on the wall of several distinguished celebrities that helped set the Silver Fox tone that we trying to create: George Clooney, Denzel Washington, Morgan Freeman, Ryan Reynolds, and David Hasselhoff. Each one represented something special: talented actor, classy guy, brawny guy, creative person, and all helped establish the swanky atmosphere we wanted to create.

In many ways, it was much tougher establishing our own eatery without the franchise infrastructure. We didn't have a construction manager, a development manager, a marketing manager, or a learning manager to help us work through the renovation process, and then once we opened, get the word out that there was a new bistro in town. In many ways, I assumed the role of construction manager and marketing manager, and I had a staff to support me.

We took over Blackstone's in December 2020, and ran it as Blackstone's for a while before closing down to renovate and transform it into Silver Fox. We wanted to stay open until New Year's Eve to take advantage of the busy holiday season, and then we shuttered on January 6, 2021.

Our goal was to start and finish the renovation in five weeks so we could open for Valentine's Day. Some would say that was foolhardy and we'd never finish in that limited time, and some would call it aspirational—and some would call it impossible. I had built up great relationships with contractors throughout the Yorkville area, and we decided to do our renovation in the middle of frigid winter. That, ironically enough, was to our advantage. Most contractors shut down in January and February when demand drops and working outdoors in the Chicago suburbs is next to impossible.

The work was interior, and because most contractors weren't busy in the dead of winter, I was able to negotiate lower prices. Since Blackstone's had lasted 17 years and the owners hadn't done any updating, we needed to do a considerable amount, creating a 360-degree bar; redoing the patio; adding a vestibule; creating a clear glass partition; establishing a private room, which we called "Foxes Den"; and adding air-conditioning. All in five weeks.

We also spent five figures to purchase a huge wood-burning grill that provides a unique, scrumptious taste to steak, lobster, and most other meats and seafood. My goal was to add the "wow" factor, so when you dig into these specially grilled steaks, your taste buds scream out, "That was delicious!"

A friend said to me, "No way an upscale steakhouse is going to work in Yorkville." But I've been dealing with skeptics my entire life, have learned not to be discouraged by naysayers and cynics, and usually pay them no mind. Since we've been in operation for more than two years now and are thriving, our success speaks for itself.

When we opened, we did a blitz of Facebook ads to let the folks in Yorkville and its environs know that we were opening a new kind of neighborhood, upscale steakhouse. We had an artist design a special rendering of the new eatery to entice guests to see what the old restaurant had turned into and to check it out and dine there.

We acquired that building for about a million dollars, and less than three years later, it has been appraised at being worth $3 million, so we're way ahead of the game.

The good news was we managed to open on February 13, a day before Valentine's Day, for friends and family. To debut within five weeks of finishing a gut renovation, in many respects, felt like quite an accomplishment. And yet something went awry that night. We saw some smoke emanating from the kitchen, and it turns out a belt had loosened on the stove, leading to a minor fire, which the fire department put out quickly.

We aimed to be the first hip steakhouse in Yorkville and also strived to be your neighborhood tavern where you could just dine on a burger and fries.

It was also a celebration for my status as an immigrant who was making it in the United States. Fewer people were asking me if I had played for the Chicago Bulls, and more people were recognizing me from a variety of articles that had been written about me in the local and business press. I was becoming known in my modest Chicago suburb. And the fact that I was born in Sudan from parents who fled Ethiopia and I was raised in a Sudanese refugee camp didn't seem to matter as much as the fact that I was making it in the United States.

At a certain point, I just felt as if I blended into the American landscape. I felt accepted, with certain exceptions. But for the most part, I was perceived as a businessperson who knew how to run restaurants, who knew what he was doing, who knew how to capitalize them and turn them into a success. What higher compliment could there be? It wasn't just Yonas, the immigrant; but Yonas, the Purple Heart winner; Yonas, the guy from Yorkville, who made it big time; Yonas, the guy who feeds us and takes care of us in times of woe. Fitting into the community was one of my most important achievements.

For me, the renovation and opening of Silver Fox was a validation of where I had been, what I had learned, what I had mastered, and what I had turned into after a decade in the restaurant industry. Every wooden beam, every tile, every barstool, was part of the overall design to bring in guests, make them feel special, and bring them back for another dinner. It showed me that being a restaurant owner, operator, and developer was what I was destined to do on earth. At least for my first 40 years or so.

One of our signature dishes at Silver Fox is the tomahawk steak, which weighs from 45 to 50 ounces, and is known as our shareable dish, depending on your appetite. Two people could share it, as could three, or often four, and still leave satiated. It is tasty and unforgettable. Our goal was to create an experience so a diner could say, "Remember that night in June when the four of us shared that tomahawk steak at Silver Fox."

In addition to that steak, our menu offered a variety of other steak options including porterhouse steak, bone-in ribeye, filet duo, and aged filet. So on one level Silver Fox was a steakhouse with other options. Although guests would choose healthy brussels sprouts as a side, several of the other sides such as parmesan fries, macaroni and cheese, and mashed potatoes were indulgences and high in carbohydrates. But that's what our audience wanted.

And we also specialized in a variety of half-pound burgers such as the Blackstone burger, topped with mushrooms; the bison burger; the pot roast burger; and the original burger. You wouldn't leave hungry after adding the fries. And there were several salad options for people who were watching their calories.

One problem was that we found that our meat costs were rising faster than we could raise prices, and that was curtailing our margins. Our solution? We decided to open the Kendall Meat Company, a local butcher shop in Yorkville that was located in a prime shopping center. Since there was a lack of quality meat and very few top-flight butcher shops in the nearby area, by starting our own wholesaler, we met the needs of our restaurants with ease. We learned from our experiences with retail trade that if you have a good product, present it in the right way, and serve the customer right, you can turn a profit. Hence, we created multiple revenue streams. The butcher shop made money, and it reduced our supply costs at the restaurants. We call that a win-win.

Operating a butcher shop is trickier in certain ways than running a restaurant. The margins are thinner, so costs need to be controlled more stringently. Furthermore, the inventory of meats has a limited shelf life. If you don't sell a cut of steak in two or three days, it loses its freshness and can't be sold. So turnaround is critical to profitability.

We also learned that people eat with their eyes. We needed to make sure that the presentation of the meats made them look appealing and tantalizing, not stale and tired. And meat prices were comparable to stock prices in terms of volatility: highs one day and dips the next. Keeping track of steak prices was consuming because of the fluctuations, so again finding the right margins to ensure profitability was one major effort. We sold everything: steaks, pork chops, lamb chops, ground beef. You name it.

Another caution: Be aware that developing your own eatery, without the brand recognition, name, and marketing skills of the larger franchising company, is fraught with traps. Hence, you'd better know what you're doing in terms of nailing down and reducing operating costs, increasing margins, finding the right location, and hiring the right staff. If any of those factors goes awry, that is, if you select the wrong location with little street traffic, or choose the wrong manager who can't meld a staff, or don't watch your construction costs and spend too much, your margins are going to be curtailed, and profit levels are going to falter.

And it doesn't matter what the business is—app, auto repair shop, or e-commerce—you'll need to wear a variety of marketing hats to get it off the ground.

Yet you can't scrimp too much, because having the right decor and look and creating an appealing atmosphere are germane to drawing in customers—and keeping them coming back for more. And you must hire the right chef to ensure that all the dishes will be appealing.

Luckily for me, I'd been in the franchising industry for over a decade. And even though I was eager to step out from it (while staying in it), use my ingenuity, and establish an independent brand, all the skills I mastered over the years contributed to making my independent ventures successful. We established a uniform training guide to make sure all employees were on board, treated customers the right way, and helped create that warm, neighborhood atmosphere we craved. It was our guide, created by us, but I borrowed the concept from the various franchises that I've worked for. If we train staff to take the coffee order and get it to the client in no more than five minutes, that plan needed to be executed. And when the party was finishing up, the staff needed to be ready to provide the check since getting the bill in a timely way is a frequent source of customer complaints in many American Express polls.

Franchises also source distributors, looking for the best product at the right price. Since I had so many connections in the industry and in this area, it was easy to find the right vendors.

But our goal was to build our restaurant business and expand it. In May 2022 we saw more opportunity in Yorkville and launched Dakotas Bar and Grill. That became our second independent bar in the area. It was more downscale than Silver Fox, and therefore attracted more of the working-class customer who wanted to dine out but didn't want to spend more than $20 to $25 a person. Many customers were blue collar, and as a dedication to my father-in-law who died that year, we installed his beloved motorcycle in the middle of the bar and restaurant as our main fixture. And Dakotas was named after my then nine-year-old son, so it was, in certain ways, an eatery dedicated to my family. We had the same chef and partners as Silver Fox, so we were beginning to be in a rhythm and growing our business.

During busy sporting events, such as college football on Saturday, Monday night football, and the World Series, it also operated as a sports bar and contained the right menu and drinks for those occasions. Our cocktail list, which included watermelon margaritas and a tequila drink with the snappy name of "El Chapo," named after the notorious drug cartel leader (a name you don't forget easily), proved crowd-pleasers as well, and of course led to higher margins than the food did. We also offered a host of appetizers and small plates such as deviled eggs and small grilled cheese bits.

Our major impetus in opening Dakotas was to provide an alternative in the Yorkville area for people who wanted to dine out but didn't want to order a pricey meal. We were located in downtown Yorkville, and this provided an escape for guests seeking a moderately priced meal (much better in quality than McDonald's), where they could take a date, order burger and fries and a beer, and get out the door with a check for $50 or so.

Like Silver Fox, we also wanted Dakotas to be a show every night. The minute you enter, you see the two huge glass cases featuring bottles of tequila and bourbon, our two signature drinks. Then you see the motorcycle and photos of the Grand Teton and the mountains of Utah, giving off that feeling of its name, Dakotas. We wanted the patron to be carried away, far from the suburbs of Chicago. We wanted the atmosphere to be hip and cool, something you couldn't get in Yorkville at the time. And that patio we constructed when the pandemic was starting so we could attract people who didn't want to dine inside? It proved to be a winner long after the pandemic started to subside.

Owning two independent eateries boosted our cash flow, strengthened our resources, and provided more employees that we could shift around. In the employment situation we were facing in the post-2020 pandemic time, having more chefs, waiters, and bartenders to tap was a breath of fresh air since hiring was becoming fraught with difficulty.

And of course, we employed many of the strategies that succeeded at the franchise level. We had special drinks of the month, two-for-one drinks, and buy this and get a second drink at a discount. All the levers that we pulled that attracted customers to our franchises also succeeded on an independent level.

Owning two eateries for us was only a starting point. Our goal was to develop four to five eateries, some new and some duplicated, each year so we'd move up to owning 20 or 30 restaurants in a two- or three-year period. And the more restaurants we had, the better the cash flow. At the same time, we were, most often, acquiring the restaurant and building our portfolio and holdings.

One of our goals was to sell out, when the time was ripe, to a larger restaurant chain or private equity group. In many ways, we were operating like a private equity group by building up revenue, opening up new eateries, increasing our cash flow, and then, in a finite period, cashing out. The idea was to grow organically until we had done everything we could to grow the business and then sell.

If we could develop the right people, the skilled managing team, a system for training new managers, and a system for ordering food that was well sourced, we put in place all the steps to keep expanding the business. It was all about having the right people and operations in place.

But I didn't want to stop there. I am developing two new restaurant concepts as we are going to press with this book. One is called Beach Life, which I am constructing in Diamond, Illinois, based on the South Beach Miami eatery MILA, which specializes in breakfast and early lunch, like the restaurant chain First Watch. Beach Life will elevate breakfast to the prominent role that dinner plays at most eateries.

I am also building Kaia Tapa in Oswego, Illinois, which is next door to Yorkville. It will concentrate on Spanish and Mediterranean tapas and some sushi. Because of the pandemic and some supply chain issues, its opening looks as if it will be delayed until 2024.

What underlies these new eateries is my eagerness to flex my muscles and break out of the predestined franchise formula. With nearly 15 years of restaurant experience, it was time for me to break the mold, explore new boundaries, and set up on my own culinary path rather than follow the predetermined, tried-and-true blueprints.

And it's not just new eateries. In 2019, a friend of mine named Kevin Delaney, who ran a floral business, wanted me to meet Sanford (Sandy) Stein, a successful attorney who was involved in certain cases regarding the new recreational marijuana law. "You need to meet the godfather," Kevin said, calling him that because Sandy knew a lot of people who could get things done in the area.

And so we did meet at lunch. We were just talking together when Sandy said that he thought the marijuana-infused liquor business was about to take off and grow.

"What if we developed our own vodka company?" I asked. "I'd like to call it 'Kountry Vodka,' with a K to signify that we were opening a brand-new territory, like a new country with a twist; hence the 'Kountry' with a K, not a C. We could build it up, and try to develop a liquor laced with marijuana, and make it a special blend."

It turns out that we never tried that ultimately. Later that week, Kevin called to say Sandy loved the idea of starting a vodka company, so let's get going. I wanted to bring in my friend Brandon, because he was a former bar owner who had all the right connections, and he agreed to join us.

We had the team in place, but we needed to create the product. Since none of us was an expert in distilleries, we partnered with people from Candella Distilleries based in Youngstown, Ohio. They worked with spirits companies to develop products. They helped us follow all the governmental regulations, get permits signed, and start to concoct our new vodka product. Since Candella was based in Ohio, we worked with a Midwest corn company, corn being one of the main ingredients of the vodka that we were making. We experimented with several blends, and then we did blind tasting with men and women since we wanted to appeal to both audiences. Finally, we agreed on one recipe that most people preferred.

Starting in 2022, we hired a distributor who specialized in small accounts, so we're sold mostly in bars, liquor stores, grocery stores, and restaurants. We're now offered in about 1,000 locations, but our goal is to triple that number in a year or so, and to achieve that goal, we've hired a new, larger distributor.

Our goal was to "own the town." That is, we wanted as many people as possible in the local restaurant and liquor business to know about Kountry Vodka, and we wanted to use the region as a stepping-stone to expand. We raised $2 million to get going and secured a board of directors to set our growth path. Once we established our name in Illinois, we started selling in Florida and are looking to extend to Wisconsin and Michigan.

Industrious Brandon tapped his many bar and liquor store connections, and literally went door-to-door letting people know about Kountry Vodka, which is classic guerilla marketing. As noted above, our goal was to own our own hometown first—make it big in Yorkville and its environs—and then expand.

How was I able to oversee 47 restaurant franchises, 2 independent eateries, a retail butcher shop, and a vodka company? One of the keys was hiring multiunit managers to oversee the restaurant franchises. The way I see it, I operated as CEO of our organization, the multiunit managers were equivalent to presidents, and the store managers served as vice presidents. In that chain of command, everyone had a job to do, with explicit goals and expectations.

Technology facilitated everything we did. We secured daily sales numbers for each franchise, analyzed them, and then discussed them in weekly calls with the multiunit managers. Everyone is communicating, devising ideas of how to boost sales, increase margins, and attract new customers. As CEO, my role is to set the tone and standards and assure that each manager attains them.

We also have cameras set up in every franchise to see what is going on, view the drive-throughs, see how the movement with customers is going, and observe how staffers are handling them. Watching the metrics helps us to reach our goals.

In addition, on my smartphone, I keep track of weather alerts at all our locations. Weather affects everything in the food business. It can lead to closing our stores, as a hurricane in the September 2022 period in the Fort Lauderdale, Miami, and Sarasota areas did. Whenever we're on our weekly manager's call, I'll ask if there are any upcoming weather movements on the horizon that can ruin or curtail our business.

These multilevel managers are critical to keeping our franchises humming and pulsating. Some oversee three stores, and some five, and some eight, depending on their level of experience. I stress having open dialogues with them, and encourage them to bring up problems and to work with me to find solutions. If they hit their margins, they receive bonuses. And I strive to treat them with respect and take care of them. They're the ones who make those franchises successful; they are the eyes and ears and pulse of every Dunkin', Smoothie King, Chicken Salad Chick, and Arby's that I own.

For me, it's all about prioritizing. Do I focus on Silver Fox or Dunkin'? Of late, I've been concentrating on building up Kountry Vodka—that is the business that is primed to explode. Changing bottling companies and working with a more potent distributor have been on my daily agenda. Still, next week that could change, and we might open a new independent restaurant or look to acquire another franchise. Every day varies.

The one trap I try to avoid is complacency—and, yes, I know I've said this before, but it is such an important point, it bears repeating. The minute an owner takes a step back and thinks everything is going well and everything is under control, the roof is ready to cave in. I always keep on my toes—always prepared to problem-solve and never take anything for granted. I call it "staying in survival mode," just the way it was when I started out and was struggling to get my new businesses off the ground. Being hungry is the way to go; if you're too self-satisfied, it only leads to a downfall.

FOR OPENING YOUR OWN BUSINESS

TIP #1
Devise a Clear Concept

Every restaurant needs a clear theme, a defined audience, a certain kind of atmosphere that appeals to a certain clientele. You can't be all things to all people, even if you're selling burgers and fries. So Silver Fox Bar & Grill was upscale, and Dakotas aimed at a more middle-of-the road audience, and the menus and atmospheres reflected that.

TIP #2
Choose the Right Partners

It's tough running a restaurant solo; too many tasks and too little time. So if you're looking for partners, try to make sure you're all simpatico, as I've been with mine. Otherwise, conflict will emerge in an instant.

TIP #3
Create a Signature Dish

Restaurants become known for a signature dish, which draws people in, creates buzz, and can boost publicity. At Silver Fox, our 45-ounce or more tomahawk steak was a crowd-pleaser and unforgettable entree.

TIP #4
Use the Protocols of a Franchise
to Run Your Independent Eatery

Franchises are strong in creating protocols for training and hiring and managing. And many of those skills are easily transferable to operating independent eateries. We established our own training guide for Silver Fox and Dakotas, and that helped create a winning team and a set of standards to adhere to. Hence, that coffee ordered better be delivered in five minutes, and servers have to keep their eyes on their guests to deliver that check speedily when the meal is over.

TIP #5
Don't Stop at One

By opening two restaurants, we could keep our costs down and appeal to a wider array of customers. And we were hoping to expand even further and cut costs more.

TIP #6
Diversify Your Holdings

Since I owned 47 restaurant franchises and often the real estate they were situated on, I thought diversifying my holdings would yield benefits. Starting a series of independent restaurants not only challenged my creativity but spread my wealth and gave me diverse revenue streams. Someone once told me that the more revenue streams, the better, so if one subsides, the other spikes up.

TIP #7
Financing Your Own Business Makes Your Life Easier

At the beginning of my business career, I depended on SBA and bank loans to capitalize my businesses. But once my businesses generated healthy profits, I was able to save and capitalize, acquire businesses, and renovate the restaurants on my own. And let me tell you, avoiding loans is a very liberating feeling.

TIP #8
Success Breeds Acceptance

When you're an immigrant starting out, everyone seems to question you. "How did you get to own the Anytime Fitness Center?" was the root of many questions. But as my reputation grew and my success proliferated, and I got written about and known in the community, my acceptance grew. Now people were delighted to see that Yonas was opening a new restaurant, rather than question why an immigrant was expanding his roster of eateries.

TIP #9
Keep Expanding with New Products

After starting the independents and still owning the franchises, I introduced a new vodka company, Kountry Vodka. Yes, it was not a restaurant, but we also owned a butcher shop and were learning a considerable amount about retail sales. Once again, diversifying product lines and introducing new revenue streams could only lead to making more money and keeping profits humming along.

TIP #10
Tap Guerrilla Marketing

To get the word out that we were offering Kountry Vodka, my partner Brandon went door-to-door to liquor stores, bars, restaurants, and grocery stores to let the world know about our new product. It was old-fashioned marketing and retro and time-consuming, but it worked.

TIP #11
Set Up a Managerial Structure

It was the multiunit managers who enabled me to expand from franchises into independent eateries. These managers ran the show, oversaw the franchises, and operated as my eyes and ears.

TIP #12
Treat All Your Employees
the Way You Want to Be Treated

I always respect my employees. If I treat them right, they give the business their all. And they know how important they are in keeping the flow operating.

PUT THIS ON YOUR WALL—OR BETTER YET, YOUR REFRIGERATOR

My Top Five Tips for
How to Succeed in Business

TIP #1
Find Your Passion

You can't fake finding your passion, and you can't be persuaded into it. It must come from within your soul, your inner workings. For me, working on my own, becoming my own boss, and becoming a problem-solving restaurateur are what enlivened me and emboldened and satisfied my core.

TIP #2
Make the Most of Every Minute

Too many people idle their time away. Distracted and forlorn, they waste their time and don't set their eyes on an overarching goal. I set my goals every day of what I need to accomplish to get the job done. Yes, I can be thrown off course by a natural disaster that strikes my restaurants, but I get back on course and do my best to make the most of every minute.

TIP #3
Use Your Immigrant Status as an Energizer, Not a Deterrent

Immigrants work hard; it's their nature. It comes with trying to achieve their goals and making a place for themselves in a new country. Respect yourself. You're as much a part of your country as everyone else. Millions of them have forged a place for themselves in their new homeland and became successful, so you're following in the footsteps of a huge mass of humanity who have adapted to life in another country. Use that energy to motivate yourself.

TIP #4
Once You Accomplish Something, Look for the Next Opportunity

If you look at the path of my success, from owning a painting-and-cleaning service, to owning a fitness center and fast-food restaurants like Dunkin' and Smoothie King, to opening a number of independent eateries, you'll see my pattern is to always look for the next opportunity. Never sit down.

TIP #5
Be Grateful for What You Have

Even when I was starting out and struggling, I felt grateful. I always knew there was a chance I could use my mettle and street smarts and savviness and succeed. In my home country, those chances were slim to negligible. Those who are cynical, negative, and self-defeating fall by the wayside. But those who are optimistic, encouraging, and positive, like me, can move up and thrive.

ACKNOWLEDGMENTS

First, I want to acknowledge the people of Tigray in Ethiopia. My people. I carry your suffering with me; I stand with you, always. I also want to thank my mom and dad, for leaving behind their entire lives, so that their children could thrive and for showing my brothers, sisters, and me the true meaning of hard work and resilience. Melissa, my favorite Dunkin OM (operational manager), your guidance has helped me countless times. Riyas, Isaiah, and my best friend, Aaron—your friendship is invaluable. To my partners Brandon, Joe, Faisal, Sanford, Kevin, Andy, Ron, TJ, and Bob—thanks for being in this with me. Thanks to the Mod Squad of Yorkvegas or Yorkville, you know who you are. Last, but certainly not least, to all my brothers in arms, 1st/AD 2/3 FA Alpha Battery—without you all, I wouldn't be the man I am now.

INDEX

Brandon (friend), 206, 207
Breakeven point, 76
Breakfast, at Dunkin' Donuts, 139
Buffalo Wild Wings, 101
Burger King, xiii, xxi, 4–6, 24, 46
  benefit of experience at, 104, 105–106, 121
  low calorie fries of, 48
  successful formula of, 65
Burgers, at Silver Fox, 201
Business
  capital for, 3–4, 9–10, 67, 189
  expansion of, 28–29
  experience failure and, 32
  growth of, 130–133, 172
  help from Chamber of Commerce of, 84
  immersion in, xiii
  internet start to, 180
  launch of, 23–29, 53–55
  operation of, 31–32
  on side of full time job, 55
Business as immigrant, key tips for, 188–191
Business expansion, key tips for, 121–127
Business ownership
  greater control and, 3, 7, 46–47, 196–197
  reasons for wanting, 53–54, 99
  traps in, 202
Business partners
  selection of, 209–210
  for Silver Fox, 194–195, 197
Business plan, 72–73, 104, 179–181, 190
Business to focus on, decision of, 208

Businesses, independent, 193–194
Butcher shop
  display at, 201–202
  running of, 201–202

Calmness, in face of challenges, 24–25, 117, 187–188
Cameras, in franchises, 208
Candella Distilleries, 206–207
Capital
  for business, 3–4, 9–10, 67, 189
  from friends, 67–68, 121, 179, 189
  from partner, 171
Capitalism, xi, 156
Career counselor, experience with, 179
Career path, for talented staff, 120–121, 148
Carol Stream, Illinois, 10
Cash flow, 173, 204–205
Celebrity photos, at Silver Fox, 197–198
Challenges, remaining calm in face of, 24–25, 117, 187–188
Chamber of commerce, help for business of, 84
Change bag in rain story, 145–146
Change in accent, assimilation and, 45
Character, staff and, 119
Chemical plant, 64–65
  supervisor, at, 97–98
Chicago, Illinois, 42, 167, 197
Chicken salad, appeal to women of, 166
Chicken Salad Chick, 165–166
  freshness of food at, 166

ABOUT THE AUTHOR

Yonas Hagos is a man from humble beginnings and has remained humble throughout his successes. He immigrated to the United States at age nine from a refugee camp in Sudan, where his parents had fled his native war-torn Ethiopia. When he came to the United States, he knew two English words: yes and no. He moved to Carol Stream, Illinois and then to Yorkville, Illinois, a suburb of Chicago.

When the World Trade Center was attacked in 2001, and he saw the country that had offered him freedom damaged, he enlisted, at age 19, in the U.S. Army. On patrol in Iraq, he was shot by a rocket-propelled grenade, nearly died, and was awarded the Purple Heart.

Upon returning to the United States, through his hard work, Yonas started exploring entrepreneurship, first owning a cleaning and painting business and then becoming an Anytime Fitness franchisee. Since he had worked as a teenager in entry-level fast-food jobs at McDonald's and Burger King, he was enamored of the restaurant business. He saved money, found business partners, and opened a Dunkin' Donuts franchise in a suburb of Chicago. Its success, based on the strategies he employed, with his team, turned him into a major franchisee at several brands. He now owns 47 restaurant franchises, including 32 Smoothie Kings, 9 Dunkin's, 2 Chicken Salad Chicks, 2 Rosati's Pizza, 1 Arby's, and 1 Nothing Bundt Cakes, and has added his own independent eateries, Silver Fox Bar and Grill and Dakotas Bar and Grill, along with Kendall Mcat Company (a butcher shop that supplies some of his restaurants) and Kountry Vodka.

With no ceiling on his goals, Yonas is looking forward to future endeavors. He is eternally grateful for his strong work ethic, the teams that help him to run these businesses, and the opportunities afforded to him by this great country.

In his spare time, Yonas loves spending time with his wife and two young kids, working out, riding motorcycles, and traveling.